CW00829120

MOM'S LETTERS

MOM'S LETTERS

It's Time to Face the Truth

Mildred M. Smith

Compiled and Edited by

Sharon Lee Smith, Ph.D.
And
Joel M. Kestenbaum, Ph.D.

ELM HILL

A Division of
HarperCollins Christian Publishing

www.elmhillbooks.com

© 2018 Mildred M. Smith

Mom's Letters
It's Time to Face the Truth

All rights reserved. No portion of this book may be reproduced, stored in a retrieval system, or transmitted in any form or by any means—electronic, mechanical, photocopy, recording, scanning, or other—except for brief quotations in critical reviews or articles, without the prior written permission of the publisher.

Published in Nashville, Tennessee, by Elm Hill, an imprint of Thomas Nelson. Elm Hill and Thomas Nelson are registered trademarks of HarperCollins Christian Publishing, Inc.

Cover Artist: B. Joy Kelly, Artist, Founder and Director of Bonfire Ministries

Elm Hill titles may be purchased in bulk for educational, business, fund-raising, or sales promotional use. For information, please e-mail SpecialMarkets@ ThomasNelson.com.

All Scripture quotations, unless otherwise indicated, are taken from the King James Version. Public domain.

All Letter entries included in "Mom's Letters" are rightfully passed on to Sharon Lee Smith of the "Sharon Smith Living Trust".

Library of Congress Cataloging-in-Publication Data
Library of Congress Control Number: 2018947099

ISBN 978-1-595558275 (Paperback)
ISBN 978-1-595558213 (Hardbound)
ISBN 978-1-595558268 (eBook)

PREFACE

Mildred Smith is the author of this book. In 1976, she received the Baptism of the Holy Spirit. It wasn't too many months after she received the Holy Spirit that she began to receive letters from the Holy Spirit.

She would sit down with a paper and pencil and thoughts would form in her mind. She would write them down, word by word as they came to her.

These were thoughts that she did not form by herself. They were on themes about which she had little or no information. They were scripturally based, although she did not know it at the time. Some of the ideas seemed strange to her. They certainly were not her ideas.

One of the most significant things about these letters was the loving way in which they were written. If the letter dealt with sin, it was presented in a manner that gave anyone reading the letter an insight regarding why sin offends God. The letter leads the reader to seek change from that sin, drawing that person closer to Jesus.

The love of Jesus is evident in these letters. As people read them they are aware of the depth of love that Jesus has for all mankind! Jesus does not condemn anyone! He calls and draws them into a daily walk with Him.

Whether a person reads only one letter a day or reads the book in its entirety all at once, his or her life will be changed. It is a labor of love sent to the people of Earth daily, except Sundays or during the times when earthly matters took precedence in Mildred's life.

Mildred was never in a trance. She could answer anyone who

spoke to her and then she could continue with the letter. She could write at any time that she chose. The Holy Spirit was there whenever she asked Him to talk to her.

These letters are just a small sample of the way that the Holy Spirit communicated with her. They are on many diverse subjects. All are related to God and the way that man relates to God. They bring wisdom and understanding about God to a world that has shut God out of daily life.

The letters are like a spiritual bath of goodness. They clean and purify one's soul as the thoughts that have been sent to each reader. God would speak face to face with the people. He is love, see Him as such!

ACKNOWLEDGEMENTS

The words of these letters are from the Holy Spirit, who dictated them to Mildred M. Smith. As in all dictations, errors can be made. Some letters were typed in advance by Burl C. Smith, Mildred's husband. In later years, some were input into word-processing documents. It was an enormous effort of joy for him. Some letters were lost in the confusion of life, moving, illness, and a fire that totally destroyed Burl and Mildred Smith's home.

We, the compilers, were the ones to edit spelling and punctuation. Wording was kept as close to the original as possible. We chose the letter headings and accompanying Scriptures from the King James Version of the Holy Bible, and we put the letters in a publishable format. Any errors are ours. Interestingly, pronouns that delineate between males (his) and females (her) were rare in the original copies. "Her" is only used when referring to a woman or women, e.g., Eve, Mary, mother; that concept is true for "his," as well. Generally, the gender is neutral, which creates an awkwardness between singular and plural agreement. In that unusual approach, we find a loving God calling, reaching out to all of mankind, but speaking to us as individuals.

It is important to acknowledge all of Burl and Mildred Smith's children, the apples of their eyes: Sharon, Steven, Jeffrey, and Philip Smith—all married, and the "boys" had children and grandchildren, whom Burl and Mildred dearly loved. They were loving and kind parents, and prayed for each and every one of their family members to be believers in Jesus Christ. They lived a Christ-centered life.

INTRODUCTION

In 1976, Mildred M. Smith received the Baptism of the Holy Spirit. Within two months, the Lord told her to "sit down and write." From that day forward, she handwrote "a letter" dictated by the Holy Spirit to eventually be shared with her family, with believers, and, finally, with nonbelievers. She normally wrote six days a week, resting on Sundays. Occasionally, she would miss a day or two, but rarely. Approximately three hundred letters were written each year for thirty-five years. The writing ended when she was in a car accident. She went directly from a few days' stay in a local hospital to an Alzheimer's unit, where she eventually died. Yes, that means for several years, she was still able to clearly hear the Word of the Lord and to write His dictation after the onset of dementia. It was only one of the many miracles that took place during her thirty-nine-year Holy Spirit inspired relationship with the Holy Trinity.

A script-bearer was assigned early in Mildred's writing, and that was her oldest child and only daughter, Sharon Lee Smith, Ph.D. Her task has now started. She and her husband, Joel M. Kestenbaum, Ph.D., are the compilers and editors. They, as did many others, watched Mildred sit and write without any preparation or hesitation. The words were always amazing, often prophetic, and always from God; that is why there is an index.

CONTENTS

It Is Time to Face the Truth!

And ye shall know the truth, and the truth shall make you free.

(JOHN 8:32, KJV)

January 1, 1999

If the Lord says I'm a blessing, then I am! If the Lord says I am salt, then I am! Whatever He would have me to be, I pray that is what I will be. The Lord knows who and what He has need of and what I should be. All too often, it is easy for a person to do that which they want to do. The Lord's work isn't always pretty or glorious. Sometimes it is abrasive.

When someone cuts their finger, the last thing that they want to do is rub salt in it. It makes the cut more sore, but there are times when someone must be abrasive if they are to startle another into action. To save the soul of someone is to get past the polite things that people say to each other. A person needs to reach down into the depths of one's understanding. They must bring the truth out for people to see.

> Everyone lies to themselves.
> They would be seen as someone who
> Has everything under control.
> No weeping willow who bends down,
> Shedding its tears onto the ground.
> Someone who sees the light of day

1

That helps one grow in every way.
Is the type of person I would be.
No weeping willow tree for me.
But here I stand on crumbling ground.
That which I have done has been unsound.
With every step the earth does shudder.
Oh, how I wish that all would change.
Let no one my image enrage.
For all that I want to be,
Should be a copy of Jesus.
Today, tomorrow, the people
On earth will gamble with life.
They will know what they should do.
They will complain about others
And their open sin.
Will they ever look into themselves?
Will they take the self-pity that enwraps their souls
And burn it away with the truth?
Then they will grow in the Lord.
Wash away old traditions
With a thoughtful mind.
Remove the weeping that is in vain.
For people are who
They make themselves out to be.

Lying never saved anyone's soul. It just makes resolution harder to do. Jesus came telling the truth. He leads people out of their self-pity into a new strength in life. One cannot hide and blame others forever. Nor can they hide in their ignorance, blaming others for who they are or what they have become. It is time to face the truth! Life will no longer be too difficult to handle when one knows how to handle who they really are.

If people fall short of their goals in life, then they can accept what they are or set about becoming who they want to be. Jesus knew what God had decreed for Him. How easy it would have been for Jesus to rebel against God and take the power He had to do as He pleased. But He set Himself on the task that was given Him, and His fulfillment laid ahead of Him.

Life Is Richer Because of Him!

Therefore with joy shall ye draw water out of the wells of sal-vation. And in that day shall ye say, Praise the LORD, call upon His name, declare His doings among the people, make mention that His name is exalted. Sing unto the LORD; for He hath done excellent things: this is known in all the earth.

(ISAIAH 12:3–5, KJV)

January 2, 1999

Let there be glory, honor, and praises unto the Lord Jesus Christ. He is mighty and has done great things for the people of earth. Those who call upon His name and obey His ways shall find that they serve a worthy Master. His teachings shall always be a strength and a blessing to them. Their stay on earth will be more pleasant by far because they have learned the secrets of life.

It doesn't just happen; it is a plan from God that people should know the ways of God. When they know Him, they live a better, fulfilled life. His ways are not too confining for those who know Him. They bring freedom from fear and want. Since the people are able to live a richer life because they are able to discern right from wrong, they can make decisions more quickly. They are able to walk a more perfect life. Trouble doesn't stalk them. Fear does not confine them, because they know that they are following after that which Jesus has perfected for them.

They know that Jesus is true and He remains ever faithful to those people who call upon His name. His assurances strengthen them—and when life seems to be too overwhelming for them, they know that, in due time, this, too, shall pass and that their faith in Jesus has proven to be true. He has never left them or forsaken them. They were grafted into His mind-set and they find Him to always be ready to embrace them in His ways.

The stories of the Bible tell about the cruel problems that people have while they live upon earth. There were times when a certain problem would press down on the people. They would suffer the most harried of circumstances. People would lose all that they had. The lives of people who were followers of God would be placed in jeopardy. In fact, many would die, but God had made a covenant with them as a people. They always had His promise that God would watch carefully over their souls.

Jesus came to earth. He was treated badly by the forces on earth. He was murdered, and so those who were in charge thought that the ways of Jesus would be erased from society. But Jesus rules still. His power has increased because, wherever there are believers in Christ, there is hope for the human soul. People are the reason why Jesus came. He is still able to save them. Life is richer because of Him.

THE GREAT HOPE AWAITS ALL WHO LOOK UNTO GOD AND WHO EMBRACE JESUS AS THEIR LORD

Little children, let no man deceive you: he that doeth right-
eousness is righteous, even as he is righteous. He that
committeth sin is of the devil; for the devil sinneth from the
beginning. For this purpose the Son of God was manifested,
that he might destroy the works of the devil. Whosoever is
born of God doth not commit sin; for his seed remaineth in
him: and he cannot sin, because he is born of God.

(I JOHN 3:7–9, KJV)

January 4, 1999

We can see more clearly now the purposes that God had for mankind. They were made in His image! They are to be reflections of Him. His purposes are made manifest in us. We are to make a society that reflects the glory and purposes of God. We have a free mind that helps us to be all that God would have us to be. He would have us be reflections of His nature.

The Heavens hold God and His court. They are at peace with each other. There is no animosity in God's people toward each other. Each is acceptable to the other because each has already received the mind that is in God. It wasn't always this way. There was a war between God and those angels who turned away from Him. They were thrown out of Heaven.

Today, there is a warfare upon earth for the souls of the people. There is much to be gained for those people who seek God and His righteousness. They will have an entrance into Heaven if they prove themselves to be righteous before God. But if they refuse to obey the ways of God, they shall be cast off, just like the rebellious angels had been cast away from the presence of God.

All who are found to be worthy will be saved, and they will share in the glory and riches of God. He will embrace them at any time they find Him. Heaven can hold all who come unto it. There is no time limit or space limit. People will one day have the freedom to come and go wherever and whenever they please. They will be unlimited in space or time.

People were not created to be like angels. They have less power on earth than the angels did in Heaven. But when a person embraces Jesus and has a change of moral character, they will be more powerful than the angels. It is through Jesus that a person makes this change. Jesus is the Son of God. He has the power of God, and those who are accepted as His brothers and sisters will receive the blessings that God has given unto Jesus.

God called Jesus His Son. As brothers and sisters in Christ, we become more powerful than the angels. They were Heavenly Hosts who had great power. Yet, that power is nothing compared to the power that God has for the brothers and sisters in Jesus Christ.

The great hope awaits all who look unto God and who embrace Jesus as their Lord. Jesus has much to teach those who search for Him and embrace His truths.

THERE ARE TIMES
WHEN PARENTS THINK THAT
A LITTLE REBELLION IS CUTE

Woe to the rebellious children, saith the LORD, that take coun-
sel, but not of me; and that cover with a covering, but not of
my spirit, that they may add sin to sin: That walk to go down
into Egypt, and have not asked at my mouth; to strengthen
themselves in the strength of Pharaoh, and to trust in the
shadow of Egypt!

(ISAIAH 30:1–2, KJV)

January 5, 1999

J esus is the rock of our salvation! His banner over us is love. He
would have people love each other, putting away all of their
grievances and be understanding of one another. Yet, He would
not have people be accepting of sin in any way.

People see childhood as a time of innocence. Children *are*
innocent, but they soon learn how to manipulate other people
to get what they want. They are selfish and self-centered in their
approach to things. They want pleasure and excitement. They
expect safety in what they do. They see their parents as the ones
who control their lives and they enjoy being the center of their
attention.

Each doting parent is required to fulfill the needs of his or her
child. It is commonly thought that there is an unwritten rule that

9

parents brought children into the world, and now they are the ones who are responsible for them. All that the child does is a reflection on the parent. If the child refuses to take any responsibility for selfish actions, is it up to the parent to cover up for that child?

There are times when parents think that a little rebellion is cute. They like to see an independent streak in their children. They feel that they are learning how to cope in a world that isn't always fair in the way people treat each other. So they like to see sauciness and rebellion, until the child uses it against their enemy and rebels.

Parents become startled at the actions of their teenager when the child refuses to listen to their counsel. A child can rebel against others, but not against the parents who love and care for them all their lives. They should always give honor to their parents! Yet, here is a parent, at an early age, allowing the child the right to rebel against the other parent, the school, and the laws of God. For when someone is rebelling, there is no sacred thing that will escape their right to rebel.

Should a child be allowed to learn how to discern between right and wrong? Yes, in a world where other people are unjust, a child must learn that not all people can be trusted. But there are times when a child must be taught the things that are right and important for their well-being. There are other times, in a controlled situation, when parents can let a child make a mistake—to see what becomes of someone who has rebelled against authority.

It Becomes More Evident Daily That True Love Is Hard to Find

And now, Israel, what doth the LORD thy God require of thee,
but to fear the LORD thy God, to walk in all his ways, and to
love him, and to serve the LORD thy God with all thy heart and
with all thy soul, To keep the commandments of the LORD,
and his statutes, which I command thee this day for thy good?
(DEUTERONOMY 10:12–13, KJV)

January 6, 1999

Jesus is the rock of my salvation! His banner over us is love. All that Jesus has done for the people of earth shows His caring for us. It becomes more evident daily that true love is hard to find. One may care for one's children, wife, or husband as long as these people behave themselves and live a good life. But when there is a disagreement, love vanishes and people find themselves estranged from those people they once cared about.

Jesus isn't this way. He knows the nature of the people. They rebel against Jesus and His ways constantly. As long as Jesus remains a type of Santa Claus to them, they support Him. If they find that Jesus demands something from them, they rebel against Him. Jesus is not a way of life anymore. People see Him as an option they can pick up or ignore at any time. No one sees His ways as the ultimate in good behavior.

Jesus is real! He is also the ideal way of life. All that is good in a person is referred to as being godly. Anything that is evil is anti-God. Today, people have taken the Word of God and twisted it until no one really recognizes what God stands for. Some people look at Jesus as another wise man, one who lived and served the people long ago. His way of looking at things no longer works in this society. There are no positives. A person can be excused for any action that they take. If it isn't acceptable to people in general, they will go their own way, doing what feels good to them.

Everyone wants Jesus to be their only hope. He is kept in reserve until they have tried all their own ideas, then they will call upon Jesus and He is to come to their rescue the moment they call on His name. When they don't receive the instant miracle that they wanted, they turn away from Jesus. They are disappointed in Jesus. They have heard all the stories of Jesus and His miracles, not only the stories of when He walked upon the earth but also all the other miracles that were done in Jesus' name.

They fail to know who Jesus is and how His nature demands something from them. They feel no responsibility toward Jesus. He is to give freely of all that He has. He is not allowed to ask anything of them. They are to be treated by Jesus as an equal at all times. That Jesus gave His life for them means absolutely nothing. Everything is given freely, no strings attached!

This Is Why People Marry the Person Who Is a Reflection of Them

Let us be glad and rejoice, and give honour to him: for the marriage of the Lamb is come, and his wife hath made herself ready.

(REVELATION 19:7, KJV)

January 7, 1999

Oh! How I love Jesus, because He first loved me! People feel comfortable around people who like them. They have things in common and they enjoy doing things together. They laugh at the same jokes, enjoy the same things, and find each other to be pleasant company. This is why people marry the person who is a reflection of them. They may know that life can be a struggle, but when one has someone with them who can help them carry the good and the bad, they feel as if they have conquered the problems that one encounters in one's lifetime.

There are times when people send out false signals to another person. They want that person for whatever reason they may have. It is a purely selfish reason. They really don't give any consideration to the fact that they may not make that person happy, that in return for the love they may receive, they give back only bitterness instead of love and respect. Pushing oneself upon someone who no longer has any true feelings for them can only change both of them into someone neither of them would have become if there hadn't been deception by one or both parties concerned.

Most marriages are unhappy. There are many reasons that this happens. All too often, one person will grow. They will be involved with a job or some other interest. If the other mate isn't interested in what is going on with their spouse, they can become boring to their mate. There must be common interests that keep a couple a unit, or they will soon become disinterested in one another.

People can change! While the couple was dating, they did things together that they both enjoyed. After they were married, if one of the spouses gave a false impression of what they really enjoyed, the other person may become bitter. That which had brought them together turned out to be a deceitful ruse. They were not really fun to be with! They had actually pretended to be someone they were not. It would leave the other dismayed—with a feeling that they were tricked into something that they didn't really want.

All is not lost. Just because people find their marriage to be uninteresting doesn't mean that they cannot restore some fun and joy into it. It will take making time for each other. One must still find it worthwhile to spend money and time with their partner. There must truly be a time of reaching out and restoring those times that brought joy. Life is too short to be dull and uninteresting.

Dear Jesus, Cause Again the Calling of the Holy Spirit to Woo the People!

I exhort therefore, that, first of all, supplications, prayers, intercessions, and giving of thanks, be made for all men; For kings, and for all that are in authority; that we may lead a quiet and peaceable life in all godliness and honesty. For this is good and acceptable in the sight of God our Saviour;

(I TIMOTHY 2:1–3, KJV)

January 8, 1999

Jesus be the Lord of all! Jesus we surrender all! Help me to be all that You want me to be! Guide me in Your ways. Let goodness and righteousness spread throughout this land. Call the people back to You and Your holy ways. Let the people know that righteousness is its own reward. Remove evil people from places of authority. Restore a love of God and country into the hearts and minds of the people.

The people have been drawn away from righteousness because they have been taking for granted that God does not hear. Nor do they think that God sees. The land is blessed with plenty. There are fine homes and a surplus of food. No one seems to realize that sin can affect a people and cause the standard of living to fall and

15

fail. They seem to think that all is acceptable. They can do as they please and no one will be hurt by their wicked actions.

But all sin weakens a nation! It gets to a point where there are few honest people with whom one may associate. They must question everything that they see and hear. No one is able to protect themselves. No one is wise enough to penetrate into the minds of those who intend to spread wickedness into the people.

There is a core of Godly people who refuse to settle for deceit. They will not embrace a wicked group or lend themselves to wicked actions. They will not sell their souls for deceit. They will seek the truth of God, for it is their life's blood. They see Jesus as the center of all life, and they will not accept another.

Jesus will honor them. He will send His blessings to them. He will recall to mind the type of people who once ruled the land and call forth those who still serve Him in honor. He will allow the land to be restored to its glorious days when these people lead the world with their God-fearing ways!

Dear Jesus, cause again the calling of the Holy Spirit to woo the people! Do not let wicked people with wicked intentions make a mockery of Your precious name. Let the people remember the goodness of their elders who stood for righteousness. Let the mothers, fathers, and grandparents be brought to mind, as they went forth to conquer a virgin land and spread the Gospel of Jesus Christ to all who would hear. Let the children hunger after righteousness and restore the righteous people back into the fabric of this nation!

WHERE HAS JUSTICE GONE?

When the righteous are in authority, the people rejoice: but
when the wicked beareth rule, the people mourn.

(PROVERBS 29:2, KJV)

January 9, 1999

Blessed Jesus, still our strength and Redeemer! In You do we place our trust! No matter how wicked the world becomes, Jesus remains steadfast in what He believes!

It is so sad to see our highest governmental officials cater to wickedness. They use forceful rhetoric to sway the people. They lie without shame or fear of being caught! They disgrace their respective offices and the trust that people have placed in them. They do not act ashamed and force themselves upon the people in a brazen way.

They accuse the people of being lethargic and not really being interested in what is happening at the highest places of government. Yet, the people clamor for truth, and those who protest the loudest are treated as if they are the ones who are causing the problems in the land! The people are supposed to remain amicable, accepting everything that is told them. Their voices are to be stilled, as those who have taken over the power in the country continue living with different rules than the rest of the people.

Law enforcement increases as each small town is encouraged to hire more police officers who badger the people into doing

17

things that are not acceptable. As the leaders become greedy and place the burden of more tax money on the people, the people are helpless to do anything about it. If the people refuse a tax raise, the leaders think of some other method to tax the people.

Where has justice gone? As Jesus has been removed from governmental consideration, the leaders have no one to keep them in check. They do not like the simple rules that have been placed on the people by laws of God. They do not trust the laws that are written on the hearts and minds of the people, making them responsible for themselves. Pain would afflict the bodies of the people, beating them into submission to the laws of governing forces!

Goodness doesn't pay the rewards that it once did. No one respects those people who would treat other people with kindness and respect. They can keep any law that they please but do not expect other people to obey the standards that others have set up for themselves. It only becomes a burden that people must fulfill by their own integrity. Each person has the right to do as they please, as long as they are able to put their ideas into action. One cannot expect others to have the same righteous ideas that they have. A single rope made of several strands is stronger, but the rope can be built by those who are evil and used for destruction instead of righteousness. Jesus never fails those people who call upon His name!

We Would Ask That There Be a Great Movement of the People Back to Jesus Christ

And in thy seed shall all the nations of the earth be blessed; because thou hast obeyed my voice.

(GENESIS 22:18, KJV)

January 11, 1999

Hear my prayer, oh Lord, attend unto my prayer! I'm thankful for the times of abundance that have fallen upon the land. Are we blessed because of time and chance? When we, as a people, have gathered together from many different countries, have we been blessed by who we are? Or is it because our land is a large, rich land that can hold its people in prosperity? As a nation, have we lived up to our motto—"In God We Trust"—so that we may receive the blessings of God as the people who believe in Him?

In all the years since we have become a nation, we have not always acted morally and justly. We have had many self-interests! We knew that we were a mighty people and that we had no quarrels with our neighbors. We have lived in peace except for the warfare that we had among ourselves. It has not been outside influence that has caused our problems but by the wickedness that was found in the minds of the people.

People from other lands have moved here. They came to a

beautiful land filled with great riches. They took that which they found here and built it into the most powerful land in the world. Some people gave us the lands that gave us wealth, and people demanded that we become a part of their lands. They tried to take us over by force, but they did not succeed. They could not, and they lost all their power to govern us when they could no longer control us! We became a country and a government in our own right!

Because we are a rich and powerful nation, the rest of the world look at us as the breadbasket of the world. They expect us to share our bounty with them. Although we are a rich nation, we got there by our hard work and belief in Jesus. We feel He has made us great and a generous people. But we are not the slaves of the world. Their lands are more massive than ours. They have many people who should be watching over their own people. They should embrace Jesus and ask for His grace to be on them.

We would ask that there be a great movement of the people back to Jesus Christ. The riches and wisdom can be theirs; there is no limit of resources in Him. We, as a people, do not care to rule the world! There are enough people and resources to support many nations. We would that all peoples support themselves and join together to make a world of goodness and peace.

THERE IS SOMETHING THAT HE BRINGS TO PEOPLE THAT THEY CANNOT RECEIVE ANYWHERE ELSE

But because I have said these things unto you, sorrow hath filled your heart. Nevertheless I tell you the truth; It is expedient for you that I go away: for if I go not away, the Comforter will not come unto you; but if I depart, I will send him unto you. And when he is come, he will reprove the world of sin, and of righteousness, and of judgment:

(JOHN 16:6–8, KJV)

January 12, 1999

Jesus is the hope of all the people on earth. There is something that He brings to people that they cannot receive anywhere else. Many people deny the spiritual aspects of people, but it is as true and powerful as one's physical awareness. As people begin to seek Jesus in their lives, they become more moral and life becomes richer, fuller, and deeper for them. There is a change in their attitude toward righteousness. They begin to have a heart toward God.

Many people see this as being foolish. They fail to realize that unseen things can affect them. They begin to resist any calling of the Holy Spirit. They do not want to be touched by the Spirit of God in any way. They feel that they are in control of themselves and resent the idea that a spirit can affect them and their lives.

Once a person receives the Holy Spirit, He strengthens that which is good in a person and rejects that which can cause a problem. He turns their hearts to righteousness. He never bullies them or causes them to hate themselves. All that He does is done in love. The person rejects evil and embraces good. They can look at themselves and be repulsed by what they did wrong in the past. Then they turn away from that sin that once called to them. It has lost its power over them. They rejoice because they are free from some sin that had blinded them to righteousness. They are free! Free to make good choices for themselves.

No longer are they held to sick things that bound them in unforgiveness. They can now say, "I forgive myself. Once I was bound by some sinful thing that would cause me fear and destruction. Now I'm able to shed that compulsive habit that kept me constantly a slave to it. Jesus has freed me. He doesn't make me do anything that I don't want to do! I want to be free from any sin that would not allow me to live a peaceful, successful life on earth."

This doesn't come about until people get to know Jesus and ask Him into their hearts. Just as a bath can cleanse the filth from one's body, so does the Holy Spirit cleanse us from sin. One joyously begins to live life anew in the presence of God. One does not see with their eyes the transformation that takes place, but they do feel it with their hearts. They cast away those things that bound them to sin and are set free!

LET OUR LIGHT SO SHINE THAT PEOPLE WILL KNOW THAT WE ARE CHILDREN OF GOD

And when he had so said, he shewed unto them his hands and his side. Then were the disciples glad, when they saw the LORD. *Then said Jesus to them again, Peace be unto you: as my Father hath sent me, even so send I you. And when he had said this, he breathed on them, and saith unto them, Receive ye the Holy Ghost:*

(JOHN 20:20–22, KJV)

January 13, 1999

Jesus be the Lord of all. Jesus we surrender all! Help us be all that You want us to be! Keep us from sin! Let our light so shine that people will know that we are children of God. Remove us from sin so that we will not be tempted to stray from Your holiness! In a world that seems to be bent on destruction, lead us to a place of peace and sustain us there! Help us guide our family so that we will be a reflection of all that Jesus can be to the people of earth.

We give thanks for the Word that God has given us, so that we can know His ways. Without guidance, we could become confused in life. There are times when we would look the other way and not demand justice, or correct behavior from those with whom we associate. We know that they are wrong, but they are determined to follow after unrighteousness. That unrighteousness could cause trouble for them, and they could lose their souls.

The people who know You have been told to go to all the world and spread the Gospel to those who have not heard about the benefits of Jesus. When people hear, they receive a heart to receive that good news for themselves. Jesus and all His goodness spread out before them to see. Then they are able to make a choice about how they can serve Jesus in their lives. It takes a while for the people to clear their minds of unrighteousness. They have been taught that people are supreme, and that they do not need to bow before anyone. Soon they receive with joy the message of Jesus Christ. Jesus can fulfill many of their hopes that they know they do not have the ability to do for themselves!

There is great joy in knowing that there is hope for fallen mankind. When a person can assess all the wicked things that they have done and then realize that there is no way that they can receive pardon for what they have done, they become remorseful for their own well-being. When they know that in Jesus they can receive forgiveness and be reconciled with their Maker, they find a reason to rejoice and change their wicked ways.

When people have received a death sentence and there is no hope of being set free from it, they are remorseful. They would give much to be able to start all over again. This is why true repentance in Jesus is so vital to those people who seek forgiveness and change. They see Jesus as their only saving grace. They are delighted to meet Jesus!

We Call Upon Jesus to Once More Stir the Hearts of the People to do That Which Is Morally Right

But take diligent heed to do the commandment and the law,
which Moses the servant of the Lord charged you, to love the
Lord your God, and to walk in all his ways, and to keep his
commandments, and to cleave unto him, and to serve him
with all your heart and with all your soul.

(JOSHUA 22:5, KJV)

January 14, 1999

We give You thanks, dear Jesus, for this great land of ours. We have followed closely the way that You would have us go. We have heard and received Your message about goodness and righteousness. Our laws have been built upon You and Your words. In this time of crisis, we ask that Your truth and Your ways will not be forsaken. We ask that justice will be done and the people will respond to the laws that have led us through other times of crisis in our country.

All too many people have seen fit to defend evil people in high places. Just like the Jewish people, when they were under bondage to the Egyptians, would come unto God and complain about their harsh slavery, so the people are complaining about the liberal ideas that have been brought into our government. These ideas

25

demean the laws of God and bring forth ideas that bring moral decay to the people.

It took God's removing the people from the land of Egypt before they could have their cries heard and changed. We do not want to return to the native lands of our origins. We are a diverse nation, made up of many nationalities. We cannot claim other lands and expect to have all the benefits that we have received in this nation. We would that the hearts of the people return to the righteousness that Jesus and His laws bring unto us. We would once again show forth the goodness that the people of the living God, Jesus Christ, display in this great land.

We seek that which is good, that which is holy, so that we can discern what is best for us and our spiritual self. We are each and every one of us of value to Jesus and to this land. To accept all manner of sin and law-breaking because someone has been put in a place of authority is not acceptable to You or us. We would see wickedness be destroyed because of evil's own weight. Sin brings a heavy burden on those who take part in it. It becomes a way of life, and people become heavily laden because they cannot reverse wickedness. At first, wickedness seems like freedom from the law. Soon, the lawlessness becomes more burdensome than the law.

We call upon Jesus to once more stir the hearts of the people, to do that which is morally right. Let all people be judged in the way that is beneficial for all people. Remove those oppressive laws that steal away our freedoms and allow that which is morally right to rule in the hearts of the people!

Jesus Knew the
Outcome of His Life

*I returned, and saw under the sun, that the race is not to the
swift, nor the battle to the strong, neither yet bread to the
wise, nor yet riches to men of understanding, nor yet favour
to men of skill; but time and chance happeneth to them all.*

(Ecclesiastes 9:11, KJV)

January 15, 1999

Let us rejoice and be glad and give all the glory unto Jesus. He
has remained true to His word. He has watched carefully over
those who are called by His name. Victory isn't always immediate,
but in the end, it is always on time!

People become nervous when they lose control of matters.
They like to know the outcome of things, so that they can make a
decision about them. They like to be assured of all the facts before
they commit themselves to a project. They do not like being
caught unprepared in a matter. But life doesn't cooperate with the
desires of the people. One must learn how to judge matters and
take actions without knowing the outcome! They have the ability
to declare, "I did the best I could, considering the amount of information that I had!"

If time and chance didn't happen to people, they would never
learn how to make decisions about matters. Their lives would be
predestined for them. They would wait until they could choose

27

that which would pay off for them. They would never test them-selves to see if they were right or wrong on a matter. It would take away their consciousness in a matter. They would always have things turn out to their advantage.

They would be selfish because they would only take the best of any situation. They would learn to walk away from anything that could cause a problem for them. They would feel superior in all their actions. They would never need to guess because the time would not be right for them if they needed to make a premature judgment.

Can one say that Jesus never needed to make a choice for Himself? He knew ahead of time what was going to happen to Him. God had let Him know the truth of the matter before it hap-pened. Could we make a decision about things if we knew we were scheduled to die if we went to a certain place at a certain time? Would we be paralyzed with fear and refuse to follow the direc-tions we were given? Would we make excuses for not showing up?

Jesus knew the outcome of His life. He truly is considered to be the ultimate sacrifice for the lives of the people. He did not fear. He moved forward, determined to fulfill the reason He was placed upon earth!

WE HAVE LOST OUR WAY!

Jesus saith unto him, I am the way, the truth, and the life: no
man cometh unto the Father, but by me.

(*JOHN 14:6, KJV*)

January 16, 1999

Jesus, Jesus, how I love Him! How I trust Him over and over. Jesus, Jesus, hear our plea! Watch and let your protection cover us with Your love! We are near self-destruction because of our attitudes toward God and righteousness. Like so many other nations in the world, the people are looking to themselves and their own personal desires, and they are ignoring the protection that Jesus and the laws of God afford us!

We have lost our way! That which is right has been made to seem wrong; the people have embraced that which is wrong. With false compassion, they embrace wicked actions in people. They protect the evildoer from the penalty of his crimes. They would join in wickedness by supporting a crime instead of reporting and rejecting any evil act.

The people are not ignorant! When they see people in high places get away with breaking the law, they do not think that the law should be followed. So they produce a lawless society. No longer can a person be trusted to follow the law because it is beneficial to them. Instead, they gamble with getting caught. If they are caught, they lie and implicate other people in their lawlessness.

29

They ruin their own lives while they cast aspersions on the very people whom they profess to love.

Have we become a society that judges the worth of a people by what they own? Does anyone live within their means so that they can become prosperous by careful planning? The things of the earth become old and corrupted. There is always something new to take its place. Does a person ever tire of wanting things that they soon cast away as unwanted things?

Jesus would be the center of one's life. He would not ever grow out of use. He is the light that draws people to righteousness. He brings contentment to the souls of the people. He lets them be satisfied with themselves, things, and friends. He makes them feel satisfied with what they have.

If one looks at others and only sees their monetary worth, one needs to adjust one's vision. It is all right to be blessed of God and to own many things. It is wrong to seek pleasures and treasures just to compete with other people.

TAKE AWAY THOSE SINS THAT CAUSE A SEPARATION BETWEEN US

But when that which is perfect is come, then that which is
in part shall be done away. When I was a child, I spake as a
child, I understood as a child, I thought as a child: but when
I became a man, I put away childish things. For now we see
through a glass, darkly; but then face to face: now I know in
part; but then shall I know even as also I am known.

(I CORINTHIANS 13:10–12, KJV)

January 18, 1999

Jesus be the Lord of all! Jesus we surrender all. Take away those sins that cause a separation between us. Help us to remain faithful in all that we do. Keep our eyes upon the prize that You have prepared for us. Although we dedicate our love and lives unto You, there are times when we grow weak and distracted from our spiritual duties. Remain ever first in our minds so that we will never waver from our assigned duty to You.

We would like to know what is to happen in the future. We want to press ahead in those areas that Jesus will bless. We want to move away from those things that will not please Jesus. We want to know, beyond a shadow of a doubt, that all that we do will receive the blessings of Jesus in our lives!

When we were children, we thought and acted as children. We needed constant guidance from God, Jesus, and the Holy Spirit.

31

There comes a time when we are no longer considered to be children. The Holy Spirit has been given the duty to teach people the ways of God. His Word is sufficient to keep us obedient to the Word of God. We should not waver, but remain steadfast in our belief in the Word. As people overcome their sin, they are to maintain that strength and then move on until they have assumed the nature of Jesus in their lives!

It is one thing to know the Word of God; it takes constant vigilance to keep it. Sin takes on many disguises. The same old sin dresses itself up in a different way, and since it can appear to be different and nothing to be alarmed about, a person can sin the same sin again. This makes their previous sin stronger in their life. Not only does it appear as if they fooled God, but that they got away with their hidden sin.

The Holy Spirit can awaken a person to the truth of sin. They can detect the ends of the sin and how it affected them. There can be joy when they escaped the penalty of sin. They can repent and have their case heard before Jesus. The sin can be erased, and they are not held accountable for that sin. They really were sorry that they sinned against God, Jesus, and the Holy Spirit.

When a person realizes that they have committed a sin, it is up to them to find out how they got involved in that sin. They are to make sure that they will not fall prey to the sin anymore. They are to study their own sinful nature and be repulsed by it. When they are adequately revolted by their own sinful nature, they will be more able to combat hidden sin in their lives!

Truth Is Far from Them

These six things doth the LORD hate: yea, seven are an abomination unto him: a proud look, a lying tongue, and hands that shed innocent blood, an heart that deviseth wicked imaginations, feet that be swift in running to mischief, a false witness that speaketh lies, and he that soweth discord among brethren.

(PROVERBS 6:16–19, KJV)

January 19, 1999

Hear my cry, Oh Lord, attend unto my prayer! We come to You for help! The people in the United States of America have lost their way! They cannot determine truth from error. They have become selfish and self-centered. They do not have the ability to discern when someone is lying to them. They accept all that they hear and do not search for the truth of a matter. They will defend a lie even though they have not bothered to check if the one who is talking to them is telling the truth.

This is a day when part of the government is bringing out their partisan spinners, who are cloaked in righteousness. They lie to the people! They take the facts and twist them to have them say what they want them to say. Uninformed people, who trust the government, will believe any lie that they are told even when the facts do not support what they are saying.

They look the American public in the eye and present a fictional

33

story that any thinking American would laugh at if they really paid attention to what was being said. With much solemnity and pride, they strut before the people, acting as if they are more intelligent and informed than the public could possibly be. But they are only echoing lies that have been told to them. They use flowery words that are supposed to cover over the misdeeds of their fellow conspirators. They do not act afraid that they will be called to answer for their malfeasance. They have the assurance of their leaders that they will be protected from any repercussions from their lies and misrepresentation of the facts.

Still the American people go about their daily work-a-day lives. They will spout out to other people as if they have heard all the facts of the matter when they have only listened to those who they know say the same things that they want to think. Truth is far from them. They cover themselves with misleading stories, so that they are not held accountable for the truth in their words.

Yet, they will be held accountable for what they have done. If their wicked devices continue, they will dictate to those who follow that lies and wickedness are profitable. As they try to find justice for themselves, they will see that a perverted justice has taken over society. They will be caught in their own foolishness while they cry for true justice.

A Little Sin Multiplies, as a Little Isn't Enough

Your glorying is not good. Know ye not that a little leaven leaveneth the whole lump? Purge out therefore the old leaven, that ye may be a new lump, as ye are unleavened. For even Christ our Passover is sacrificed for us: Therefore let us keep the feast, not with old leaven, neither with the leaven of malice and wickedness; but with the unleavened bread of sincerity and truth.

(I Corinthians 5:6–8, KJV)

January 20, 1999

Let the words of my mouth and the meditation of my heart be acceptable unto You, my Lord Jesus! Let only goodness and praise be heard! Let me be a reflection of Jesus to all the people on earth so that they may see the truth and wonder of Him.

All too often people proudly declare that Jesus is their Savior but act as if they serve someone else. They do not reflect all that Jesus stands for. To believe in Jesus means that the things that they do have been determined! Jesus made His stance on life and behavior known to the people. He did not waver! He spoke freely of the things that were considered righteous in the eyes of God. He openly declared the things that were sinful to be unacceptable to anyone who became one of His. People cannot declare that

35

they are a child of God and refuse to be as He is. People must take on the attitude and character of God.

"Oh, I just love my neighbor!" people may exclaim. But do they? They see the way others live their lives. They know those lifestyles can't be acceptable to Jesus. Are the people condemning others? No! If people know the ways of Jesus, they know if others' behaviors are acceptable or not.

There are those who declare that they like to be seen in places that they know are a bad influence on people. They like to take part in some activities that go on there. They would say that they are only having fun. That they could not lose their soul by the way they act! But it isn't too long before they take another step in the wrong direction and accept something that they would have previously thought to be wrong.

A little at a time, they cover their righteousness over until they have become someone that they don't recognize. They chase after sin in a gleeful way. It is fun, self-satisfying, and they declare that no one is getting hurt by their actions. They lie to themselves and try to involve others, so that they will have a companion in crime. It isn't any fun if you can't discuss the excitement with others. So they tell all who will listen about the fun and excitement that their little adventures give them!

There is no sin that cannot grow larger as one seeks more excitement to make life more adventurous. A little sin multiplies, as a little isn't enough. Yet, they would declare that it isn't sin. It isn't until sin gets out of control that one wishes they could return to innocence!

Jesus Has Already Declared That the Law Is Written in One's Heart

Which shew the work of the law written in their hearts, their conscience also bearing witness, and their thoughts the mean while accusing or else excusing one another;)

(ROMANS 2:15, KJV)

January 21, 1999

Jesus is Lord! There is no other person whom we can trust. Those people who would lift themselves up to be a ruler over us fail miserably to do the job that leadership demands! Do we need rulers? If coordination is needed so that people can live a prosperous life on earth, leaders are needed to program it. But those who are placed in charge all too often listen to each other instead of doing that which will benefit the nation.

Jesus knows the hearts of the people. He would have them judge correctly, so that they would live a good life on earth. But they are all too often led by their emotions instead of the righteousness of the law.

Not that the laws are always good. Laws are a means that society has to control the people. If there is a law that declares, "Thou shall not," and a person breaks that law, they are then subject to the penalty of the law. If there were no laws, then there would be no one who could be apprehended for breaking a law.

Jesus has already declared that the law is written in one's heart. This places all the responsibility upon each person to keep the law. One automatically knows when they are doing what is right or wrong. But there are man-made laws that people place on themselves. These laws govern nations. Each nation has certain peculiarities that the people of that nation want followed. They demand laws so that they are protected from those people who refuse to recognize laws. Each society has people who don't recognize the goodness of the law. They have no problem breaking the law if it interferes with the things that they want.

It is true that a person is a law unto themselves. Where they have set a standard for themselves, they do the best they can to live by their own standards. They are to sort out the things that they do, and then decide if they are good or bad. If they want to be a good person who is able to live with themselves, they follow their code of ethics.

There are times when a person gets into a collision course with one's own values. Up to a certain time, their values served them well. If they find that their standards are either too high or too low, they are able to adjust their standards. One must check back to see why one set a standard before they change it. If it has been successful in the past, they should remain steadfast in that standard.

EVEN WITHOUT ANY COMPETITION, ADAM AND EVE WANTED MORE

For whosoever will save his life shall lose it; but whosoever shall lose his life for my sake and the gospel's, the same shall save it. For what shall it profit a man, if he shall gain the whole world, and lose his own soul? Or what shall a man give in exchange for his soul?

(MARK 8:35–37, KJV)

January 22, 1999

Lift Jesus higher! Lift Him up for the world to see. If we lift Him higher, then the world will be attracted to Him. Everybody needs help in some way. They always have a need. It was only in the Garden of Eden that love existed like God had intended. People became avaricious and wanted to have more than they could supply. There is never an end to "wants"!

Even without any competition, Adam and Eve wanted more. They had never understood how bad people could be. They lived in absolute plenty, without effort of any kind from them. They had freedom to do as they pleased. Although they knew the thoughts of God, it wasn't a struggle for them to do them. Indeed, they loved God and had no true desire to offend Him. Not because they feared Him, but because they "cared" for Him!

This "caring" is a gift from God to the people. Today, the people are becoming so self-centered that they find it hard to care for other people. They want things for themselves! They don't care about anyone else. It is their desires that come first. When they get the prize, then they find fault with it. The glory was in the securing of the object, not that they really needed it for their lives' sake.

So we must lift up Jesus as the most desirable thing that anyone could possibly want. The idea that He is "free" and available to anyone who asks can make Him of little value to those who are seeking only rare and expensive "things"!

Jesus is not a "thing"! He is a way of life. It will cost people their lives when they find Jesus. He comes into them and floods them with new ideals. He is richer, fuller, and deeper! He makes life new. Things of the past, good or bad, are pushed away, as people see their souls become the most valuable possession that they have.

The soul is theirs, but now they enter into the battle that determines where their soul shall be for eternity. It isn't a one-time battle, but a lifelong one. There will be many times when some sneak thief would steal away their thoughts, striving to steal away their soul.

Because people are the way they are, they may be tempted! They may set Jesus aside for a while as they reach out for something that gives them a variety of pleasure. They soon find out that they have placed their most precious gift in danger. They repent and turn again unto the One who has placed them in a Garden of Eden. Although they fall, Jesus has made it possible for them to return to Him!

Jesus Arose from the Dead!
He was Accounted Innocent by God!

For he hath made him to be sin for us, who knew no sin; that
we might be made the righteousness of God in him.

(II CORINTHIANS 5:21, KJV)

January 23, 1999

Blessed be Jesus, the Lord of all. He has been tested by fire and He has been found innocent of all accusations. God declared Him pure, there are no faults found in Him. But people, because of their wicked hearts, have condemned Him and made Him pay the ultimate price! Death on a cross—cruel—saved for the most heinous of criminals!

Today, people are still searching for justice. They are not perfect, and there are times when innocent people are made to pay the penalty of a criminal. There are courts where a person may ask for a new trial. Sometimes, they are proven to be innocent. They are set free.

There was no higher court on earth where Jesus could appeal. He didn't even try to defend Himself from the charges. He knew that this was why He was born, so that He could bear the burden of sinful mankind. There were those who knew Jesus, and He was loved by them. They had seen Him daily. They knew all the wonderful things that He had done for them. They would have cried "Innocent, innocent!" but they cowered in fear. The tide of approval was against Him and they feared for their lives.

Jesus arose from the dead! He was accounted innocent by God! The people of earth can clamor all that they want to against Him, but His place has already been prepared for Him. His Kingdom is yet to come, and it will be filled by those who have believed in Him throughout the ages!

Those who were merciless, who called for His blood, have their place prepared for them also. Jesus is the Son of God, and His death will be atoned for by Him. Jesus did not raise His voice in protest against His accusers, but they knew that they were crucifying an innocent man. One cannot escape the blood that they have on their hands. The blood of innocent people cry out beyond the grave.

Death is the end of matters on earth, but it is only the beginning for one's soul. This has been accomplished by Jesus! Because He was an innocent man who went about doing good things, there is no one who can prove a case against Him. He has done for mankind that which people cannot do for themselves.

Today, we look back at an innocent Savior. There are still those people who call out, "Guilty, guilty!" against Him. They, too, shall be held accountable for what they have done. Just as Jesus saves those who call Him innocent, so does His blood condemn those who refuse to accept Him!

HE HELPS PEOPLE SEE
THE VALUE IN THOSE PEOPLE
WHO ARE AROUND THEM

All things are full of labour; man cannot utter it: the eye is not satisfied with seeing, nor the ear filled with hearing. The thing that hath been, it is that which shall be; and that which is done is that which shall be done: and there is no new thing under the sun. Is there any thing whereof it may be said, See, this is new? it hath been already of old time, which was before us.

(ECCLESIASTES 1:8–10, KJV)

January 25, 1999

We give You thanks, dear Jesus, for all the good things that You have given us. We feel rich beyond belief. If we would compare the things of the world to our possessions, we would find that our riches are not made up of "things"! Our richness is in You, God, and the Holy Spirit. We have better health, a positive outlook, and a feeling of satisfaction and peace. These are only given unto us by the Trinity, who meets all our needs!

We always have certain matters that take our time and attention. Living in the world and taking part in society only means that "things" are necessary. We see them as tools of the time. They, too, will become antiquated and remain as a relic to the time when they were once considered important for society to own.

Jesus is for all time. His values are such that they never grow old. They are new with each person who embraces them. They may put on a different look, but their values are eternal. He brings love and consideration to others. He helps people see the value in those people who are around them. He is always a rich source of contentment. He is peace!

Too often, people see the things of earth as too valuable. They need them now. They always want the newest of things. One would not place an article on the market that no one would want. They let people know the value of their product.

That product can help society work faster, more efficiently. It can change the way people do their jobs. But it is the value that is found in mankind that makes anything successful. Everything is made for mankind to use. In them is found the value of God. No matter how society reacts to things, it is the people who make new "things" work.

People still are the reflection of God. They are capable of doing great things because God instilled that ability in them. We can become excited because we know that we are fulfilling that greatness that has been placed in mankind.

Jesus wasn't concerned about the things of the time. His job was to show people how they are to cope with one another. They are to reflect goodness and compassion to other people. Jesus is to be our reason for living and bringing help to those we meet!

THERE IS NO PLACE TO HIDE, FOR THE TIME OF JUDGMENT IS UPON US

For the time is come that judgment must begin at the house of God: and if it first begin at us, what shall the end be of them that obey not the gospel of God?

(I PETER 4:17, KJV)

January 26, 1999

Jesus be the Lord of all! Jesus we surrender all! Help us to be all that You desire Your people to be! Do not grow weary with us, but send people with a strong word and Your wisdom to lead and guide. Give the people an ear to hear all that You are telling them. We have turned away from You and are hoping that no one will really care what we do. But there are some of us who know that we cannot live without You. We need Your wisdom daily. Hear those who know You and who want to do Your good will.

Jesus came! He gave His life for us! We need not copy that which He did as a Savior. But, somehow, the people do not hear the truth of the matter. They are following after wickedness and have complained because they are miserable! Do they know that God can help them? Are they aware that they are building a wall between themselves and God? The very same God who can help ease their pain?

We see Jesus standing alone by Himself on a dark and dreary day. There is a wind blowing that brushes against His clothes. His hair flutters in the breeze! He does not smile. He seems to be utterly alone! We notice that He stands on a hill. It seems as if He stares into space, not seeing anything that is going on around Him. Indeed, He seems absolutely all alone as He looks across the horizon!

Now our vision shifts. We see Jesus from the view that casts our gaze to the land in front of Him. There, on an opposite hill, are people. They are all grey! Their clothes are nondescript! Their eyes are haunting, imploring, pleading up unto Jesus. They are not weeping; it is a silent pain. They do not utter a word. All is quiet as Jesus surveys them.

All of them know that they are to be judged. Will Jesus really see inside them? Will they reveal to Him who they really are? Everyone knows that they will tell their own stories, of what and who they are without having to say a word. At this time, they are at the mercy of Jesus. His face does not reveal compassion, anger, hurt, or rejection. He is solemn. Where is the joy that should come from a people who have obeyed God?

The wind has stopped; still there is a hush. Each person waits; they know that they are not innocent before this perfect man. In their hearts, they are thinking, *Can He really find forgiveness for me? Would I forgive myself of any of the wicked things that I have done?* There is no place to hide, for the time of judgment is upon us. We stand silent before Him; do we judge ourselves? Have we done it in time to save our souls?

Jesus Will Have His Martyrs throughout Eternity

And cast him out of the city, and stoned him: and the witnesses laid down their clothes at a young man's feet, whose name was Saul. And they stoned Stephen, calling upon God, and saying, Lord Jesus, receive my spirit. And he kneeled down, and cried with a loud voice, Lord, lay not this sin to their charge. And when he had said this, he fell asleep.

(ACTS 7:58–60, KJV)

January 27, 1999

Jesus, You are our strength from day to day. We place our trust in You. No matter what appears to be happening with the rest of the people on earth, we must keep our eyes singularly upon You. You are in control! People run about, trying to satisfy themselves with receiving the smallest of comfort from the world. Those people who trust in You find life to be satisfactory in every way. You make them secure and strong in You.

There are people who think that money is the answer to all things. But You have told us that money can be a snare and a trap, that people are to make their natures like Jesus and to be upright in all that they do. You have told us that they will find satisfaction in following after the ways that God has given to us.

There have been many people who have given themselves for a cause. They feel that even their lives are on the line when it

47

comes to supporting their beliefs in a matter. If the cause is good enough, they will take a chance with their lives. If they win, then they have changed life on earth for many people. If they lose their life, then they feel as if they gave it a chance and maybe someone else can continue to build on their efforts!

Jesus gave His life. There are many who followed Him and His beliefs. They do not feel that anything they did was in vain! For centuries, people who believed in the cause that Jesus began were willing to face danger so that they could be counted to be one of His. Life was precious to them! Many have died supporting the ideas of Jesus. They would gladly bow down before Jesus, again and again, to show how sincere they really were to His cause!

Jesus will have His martyrs throughout eternity. They will live forever with Him. There has always been a religious struggle among people. They believe wholly in what their religion teaches. Sadly, however, the doctrines that people embrace aren't always of value to them for their spiritual life! They can be drawn away to serve where Jesus has not called them to serve. If there is failure, then it may be the organization that they serve that must answer for that failure.

We would receive the wisdom that we need in order to follow closely what Jesus would have us to do. We would not chase after someone else's dream if Jesus isn't there. We would serve Jesus with valor, in truth, when He calls us to duty!

IT IS AT TIMES LIKE THIS THAT PEOPLE CALL ON THE LORD JESUS FOR HIS HELP

For if God spared not the angels that sinned, but cast them down to hell, and delivered them into chains of darkness, to be reserved unto judgment; And spared not the old world, but saved Noah the eighth person, a preacher of righteousness, bringing in the flood upon the world of the ungodly; And turning the cities of Sodom and Gomorrah into ashes condemned them with an overthrow, making them an ensample unto those that after should live ungodly;

(II PETER 2:4–6, KJV)

January 28, 1999

Come bless the Lord, all ye children of the Lord! Who stand by night in the house of the Lord! There are times when the people are forced to recognize that there is someone who is greater than they are. They do everything possible to control their situation, but all they can do is stand. Events and times swirl about them, and all that they can do is ride out the event.

It is at times like this that people call on the Lord Jesus for His help. Stand or fall, they cannot determine it by their own power. They are at the mercy of events bigger than themselves.

Time does seem to heal all things. A person may look back at some global occurrence and be horrified by what they see. They wonder how the people survived such an ordeal. They wonder in hindsight why the people allowed themselves to get into such a predicament. As they study the events that led up to that time, they can see how all this horror could have been headed off, and the horror would not have proceeded to the detriment of the people.

The only thing that would be missing is the mind-set of the people at the time, those leaders who had already determined what they wanted to see done. It might not be for the good of the people. It was a cleansing of the land against others who had a different mind-set than theirs. They wanted to change the minds of the people, but they needed to eliminate the thoughts of the past to bring about this change!

To expedite their agenda, they needed to eliminate those people whose thoughts were different than theirs. If mass murder was all that could be done, they would do it! They were in the process of changing society, and people do not change easily the ways that they have been taught.

One would suppose that right is always right. But a group of righteous people will not allow wickedness to take place in their land. They object to their rights being taken away from them. They see how people in power want to change the way a certain group of people live. So the leaders go about determining how they will bring about their agenda on the masses. If they place fear into people, they may force them into obedience. If the people still object, they use other methods to change the minds.

They Want to See
Justice Take Place!

I have done judgment and justice: leave me not to mine oppressors.

(PSALM 119:121, KJV)

January 29, 1999

Come bless the Lord, all ye servants of the Lord! Who stand by night in the house of the Lord! There are times when the children of God pray and their intercession can go late into the night. They can be placed on a "watch," where they seek the face of God for troubling matters that have been brought to their attention. They know that, by themselves, they cannot change that which is taking place. They are confident that with Jesus' help, the situation can be remedied.

Their hearts ache for righteousness! They want to see justice take place! Even those people who have been forced to do the will of someone else for evil, inwardly like to see justice done. Their minds tell them that they can suffer a great loss if they do not go along with the wicked plan. Yet, they want someone to stand up and declare that justice should be done! They want to be swept away by the righteousness that brings a people closer unto Jesus.

They wait! Do they come unto Jesus and ask Him to do that which they have failed to do? They may even pray that righteousness is done and that they do not have to get involved with the matter. They want to be released from their tortured minds that tell them true justice will win out. But they are so enwrapped in a blanket of fear that they do not let their true feelings be known to those who have control over them.

Jesus has warned people that this is a true danger! That people should not keep company with wicked people, who will eventually involve them in evil matters. If they do not think that they can resist temptation, then they should not place themselves in danger! Is this saying that a person should never try to change a wicked trend that is polluting their living conditions? No, it is saying that if a person feels that they have enough strength to resist wickedness, they should try. They should enlist other people to their cause. They should stand when they can and yet remain faithful to righteousness.

Fear is a powerful spirit that can sway people to do things they would not like to do. When fear joins in with greed, a person may start to look away from righteousness. When discovery doesn't seem likely, a person may be willing to give up their principles on one issue. Soon, they would come to accept many things that people would perceive as evil, things that they themselves were once adamantly against. They have become corrupt.

You Assure Me and Give Me Absolute Love

And we have known and believed the love that God hath to us. God is love; and he that dwelleth in love dwelleth in God, and God in him.

(I JOHN 4:16, KJV)

January 30, 1999

You are the delight of my life! You are with me day and night! There isn't any secret that can be withheld from You! My life is rich and full because You guide me in every way. Am I controlled by You so that I'm unable to function if You aren't with me? No! You assure me and give me absolute love. I trust in the way that You have guided me. Absolute trust makes us one. You love me without smothering me with Your presence! You are God, Jesus, and the Holy Spirit!

For some reason, the people in the world fear You! People gather together to bring harm to the people who trust You. They call Your followers "fanatics" because they refuse to disown You. They have found peace in You and they know there is no other one whom they can trust with their lives. For richer, for poorer, in sickness and in health, You are the One they trust. They talk to You and feel assured that You will meet all their needs.

Life is precious to them! They would live a long and peaceful life in Your care. They would bring glory unto the One who brings them into security. How can people be secure when they live in a world that hates and despises them? There is no peace when other people hate and misuse them just because of their religious beliefs.

Jesus brings strength because He has given people the assurance that this life is only the beginning of life with Him. He lets people know that they can trust Him! When they are under persecution, He strengthens them from the inside and helps them build a character that is solid. When the winds of adversity blow, they will remain rooted in Him. Life may be blown away, but life with Jesus continues!

Some people wonder if this type of life really has any value to it. For if one must be constantly at war with others, there is no peace for them. We would ask that there be a wall of protection placed around Your children. We pray that they will grow in the wisdom of the Holy Spirit, so that He becomes a living fire inside of them, and that He will burn away the conflict that angers others, so that they can bring peace to those who have fear of them.

One only needs to know the true nature of Jesus to find the security that He has for them. They do not need to push away those who bring animosity with them; they need to reach out to gather them into the fold. Jesus embraces all who call upon His name. We love You, dear Jesus. Never leave or forsake us!

THEY CAN LIVE A RICH,
FULL LIFE ON EARTH

Lay not up for yourselves treasures upon earth, where moth and rust doth corrupt, and where thieves break through and steal: But lay up for yourselves treasures in heaven, where neither moth nor rust doth corrupt, and where thieves do not break through nor steal: For where your treasure is, there will your heart be also.

(MATTHEW 6:19–21, KJV)

February 1, 1999

B lessed be the name of the Lord! Jesus is His name! Jesus is the name of the Lord. Famous people like to go forth among the people, to hear the adulation of the crowd. They like to hear people whisper their names, as if someone who is above reproach is passing by. They do not want to be bothered by the inquisitive commoners. They do want their attention and admiration.

Unless a person understands the way the wealthy live, they cannot grasp how fearful these people really are. They have risen to the top of society, they can afford all the things that the world can offer them, but they do not always understand how to cope with life!

The common folk with all their problems and wants can bring peace and goodness to their families. They can be as well-mannered as the rich. They may like other people and have many friends. They can live a rich, full life on earth. Jesus may know them, and they may know Him. To know Jesus is to know that goodness and peace can come to everyone—rich or poor!

Then why are there so many unhappy people? Why do they strive for the "things" that other people have? "Things" are important in everyday life. Each person may declare that they have a need for the same thing that their neighbor has. These "things" define a society. A "thing" can change the way a society lives.

One may own these "things" and find them to be helpful. If people are cut off from the "things" of the times, they may find their lives to be at a disadvantage. These "things" define their culture. They will be able to communicate with the rest of the people because they are aware of the "things" that are driving their culture.

It can be difficult for poor children to compete with others who have material advantages, although it doesn't mean that they will be lost to society and remain poor.

No matter when a person is born, Jesus can be an advantage to them. If they are taught the values that Jesus taught, they can learn to cope in society no matter what the culture of the times happens to be. Jesus enhances society. He brings goodness and grace. He shows the people that there are many dimensions to life!

JESUS HAS ALREADY GIVEN THE LAWS IN A MATTER

For unto us a child is born, unto us a son is given: and the government shall be upon his shoulder: and his name shall be called Wonderful, Counsellor, The mighty God, The everlasting Father, The Prince of Peace. Of the increase of his government and peace there shall be no end, upon the throne of David, and upon his kingdom, to order it, and to establish it with judgment and with justice from henceforth even for ever. The zeal of the LORD of hosts will perform this.

(ISAIAH 9:6–7, KJV)

February 2, 1999

Let God arise and His enemies be scattered! Let God, let God arise! This is a prayer and a hope that God will arise and bring forth justice across the land. There are too many people who see religion as worthless. They call upon God in their time of weakness, but that which causes their problems never seems to diminish. They feel weak and defeated by their enemies!

It isn't as if a person wants to go to war against anyone. When some wicked person can cause problems for others, the righteous people call upon Jesus for assistance. They are aware that if wickedness gets a position of authority, they will be subject to the wickedness. It horrifies them that there is no one in authority who can stand forth and bring down the wickedness!

The people want justice! Although justice seems to be taking a beating now, they would prefer that righteousness prevails. If bad things can continue to happen to good people, their trust in Jesus diminishes. They have declared themselves to be followers of Him. As followers, they depend upon Jesus to protect them in times of trouble.

The way they can determine that wrong is wrong and right is right, is by the laws that Jesus gave to His disciples. The way that Jesus met adversity guides them in their ideas. If Jesus declares that something is true, then they believe it and will fight to defend His principles. They also expect to see justice done because everyone is aware of what righteousness really is!

They depict justice as being blind, that she cannot see the truth of a matter. Justice must listen to all the witnesses who come before her. Since she must depend upon what the witnesses say, she really can only use her best judgment in the matter.

Jesus has already given the laws in a matter. It is up to the people to judge the truth. As Jesus spreads forth His goodness for all the people to see, people are expected to choose that which is true and just. If the people, through selfishness and ignorance, refuse to be just, then are Jesus and His teachings invalid? People make a law viable! No matter how good it is, if the people will not accept the law, there is no one who can enforce it.

The laws of Jesus bring equality to all people. His laws are easy to obey. These laws do not always please the ways of the people. The people would despise the law. They would serve injustice because of their sinful nature!

People Were Given the Ability to Change

For I am the Lord, I change not; therefore ye sons of Jacob are not consumed.

(MALACHI 3:6)

February 3, 1999

Trust in Him, Jesus the Lord. At a time when people can't trust in anyone, Jesus is there! He has been faithful from the very beginning! He has always been the same! From the moment He set out to serve God and mankind, He has not failed in His duty!

The words that He spoke from the very beginning remain true. He has not changed the way that He looked at things from the start. People begin with one philosophy and evolve over the years. It all depends upon how they make it work for themselves. They place themselves and their feelings first. That which will serve them best becomes their way of life.

People do not have the ability to know how life will develop. They are capable of learning new ideas. Some ideas are an improvement; some will alter the way they go about living their lives. People were given the ability to change. This is good, because people can learn how to chart a new course from one that was failing them.

People like to learn. They grow each day in some way. Just a small incident can make a big difference in the way they handle their lives. All want to improve in some way. It can make them better people, breaking away from the foolish acts of the past. They feel renewed victory in their lives. They can be better; they can conqueror those acts that made them vile, even to themselves.

Jesus knew from the very beginning what His job would be. He knew the blessings and the curses that would be placed upon Him. He also knew that He would be the Savior of the people, even when the people had no real idea about why He was sent.

People are always looking for someone who can make their lives better. They want someone who can answer their questions. They want their problems solved quickly and easily. They want them resolved by some simple word that will change their lives and make them fresh and new. They do not really want to answer for their past. It is gone! They are changed! But what brought them to this point? Inside, they are the very same people they were before because they never made the revisions needed to make their lives better.

Jesus didn't need to change. He has the true answer from the beginning, and He has the true answer for all who seek Him!

THEY DO NOT HEAR THE WARNINGS, THAT THEIR FREEDOM IS IN DANGER

I know thy works, that thou art neither cold nor hot: I would
thou wert cold or hot. So then because thou art lukewarm,
and neither cold nor hot, I will spue thee out of my mouth.

(REVELATION 3:15–16, KJV)

February 4, 1999

Hear my cry, oh Lord, attend unto my prayer. There is a dearth of true justice in the land! There are many who demand justice, but they are working toward a false justice! They look the other way and would support evil when, in their hearts, they are aware of the injustice that is being done. They go about the nation with their tale of woe that isn't really woe. For they have perjured themselves, trying to convince the common people that they are victims!

Those brave people who have stepped forward demanding true justice fear for their lives. They have shouted from the rooftops that people are trying to steal their freedom from them. They have tried to provoke other people to stand up for true justice. The people seem to be deaf to their words. They feel powerless to come forth and demand change. They are constantly battered by lies and harsh judgments that have no basis in fact.

Still there are those who come forth bringing messages of truth. Everyone seems to be too busy to care. They do not hear the warnings: their freedom is in danger. Besides, they do not believe that injustice will prevail. They have heard of heroes who have stood up for freedom and righteousness, and have won the day. Who would ever make a villain into a hero? Everyone knows what true justice really is, don't they?

It is true that people question what true justice really is. They declare that justice is a matter of degrees. They can accept certain things, but they want to remain neutral. They do not want to cause any hard feelings, so they water down any strong justice. They do not have the stomach for a long, drawn-out battle! They want others to do their fighting for them.

Heroes? Does anyone recognize heroes today? Are they still around? Do people really care enough to support a moral cause? If asked, would they be able to tell what constitutes a good cause? But they speak in theory only! If asked to defend their opinion, they wouldn't want a heated debate. They would let someone else carry the burden, all the while cheering them on. They would remain neutral, supporting the winner.

Scripture declares that people be either hot or cold. Lukewarm people are spewed out! What is worth defending? Where are the battle lines drawn?

Integrity Is a Thing of the Past

Thus saith the Lord of hosts; The children of Israel and the children of Judah were oppressed together: and all that took them captives held them fast; they refused to let them go.

(JEREMIAH 50:33, KJV)

February 5, 1999

Come and let us go unto the mountain of the Lord, unto the house of our God. There we will bow down before Him and ask for forgiveness of our sins! Will He hear us, or has He become so angered with us that He will allow us to suffer through our times of repentance? People may say that they are sorry when they are being punished, but will they really care? They have denied God and all the things that He has stood for. In so doing, they plunge themselves into a dark and cruel condition from which they cannot escape.

They are sorry that they are being held captive by wicked people. They are not strong enough on their own to repel all the wickedness that is engulfing society as a whole. They know that they are unable to hold back the tide of wickedness. They may even declare that they knew all the time what was taking place, but they thought that some hero would ride forth and bring justice back to the land!

It would have taken many people, stirred up in anger, to bring about true justice. The people felt incapable of changing anything.

In anger, they complained to those who would hear them, only to be rejected as being too sensitive! Justice would win out, they were told. Everyone knows that if something is evil, it will not stand. But people forget that they are the rulers of the world. They either make their society good or it falls into ruin and decay.

When nations have just laws, they will stand firm. When law becomes a joke and only a few are held accountable for what they do, the land deteriorates. There is no one that the people trust. They see everyone else as a threat to them. They are not able to depend upon righteousness. They are expendable, and no one is strong enough to stand by themselves. Integrity is a thing of the past. They cower in fear, because there is no true standard in the land.

The weak are the ones who suffer the most. They are unable to cope with those who would take advantage of them. They cannot depend on anyone to take up their case. Instead, they are perceived to be expendable. They do not have enough strength to stand against the wickedness of the times. When a people take the Trinity out of their society, everyone suffers!

In Society, Each Person Thinks That They Have Certain Rights

Then Pilate said unto them, Why, what evil hath he done? And they cried out the more exceedingly, Crucify him. And so Pilate, willing to content the people, released Barabbas unto them, and delivered Jesus, when he had scourged him, to be crucified.

(MARK 15:14–15, KJV)

February 6, 1999

Could the people of earth stand under the pressure of perfect law? If they were held accountable for all that they do, would anyone be found innocent? Even those people who would declare themselves to be righteous, would they be able to stand under the glaring light of perfect subjection to the law?

As Christians, people can be excused if they are not aware that they have broken a law. When they do find out that they have broken a law, they are held accountable for the law that they have broken. If possible, they are to redeem the time and make repentance for breaking that law.

No one wants to obey the law at all times. When a person finds that the law seems to be unjust in their situation, how do they get around obeying the law? In all cases, the law was made to guide a person in their lives. They are to obey the law as accurately as possible. One may err in judgment, thus breaking a law. When they recognize that they have broken the law, they can repent and never do it again.

If they were not caught breaking the law, their minds may be set at ease. They have been fortunate that they were not held accountable for the law-breaking. One will never know when ignorance of a law can affect their lives. In the past, present, or future, breaking a law can destroy a person's life.

One should always be mindful of the reason why there are laws. In society, people think that they have certain rights. People may not agree on whether a law has been broken. God gave laws so that people could maintain a peaceful, law-abiding society—one that could call a chronic lawbreaker to task. It protects both the lawbreaker and the person who may be the victim of the lawbreaking.

It is common practice among people to twist laws to their own liking. "Did I actually say such and such? Or did you imagine that is what I said?" Someone who is trying to escape the penalty of their wrongdoing will cloud the issue, so they will not be held accountable for their actions! They may even make the people who have been the victims seem as if they are lying and are troublemakers.

Scripture gives us an example of this! Jesus did nothing wrong! He showed unusual powers and kindness to the common person, but there were those who had legal power and wanted to destroy Jesus. They set about to entrap Him using the law. They twisted the law, so they could bring Jesus to trial in order to eliminate Him and the devotion the people had for him. The law did not bring about justice!

HOW DARE ANYONE TEST THE TEACHING TO SEE IF IT IS TRUE OR NOT?

That which is altogether just shalt thou follow, that thou mayest live, and inherit the land which the LORD thy God giveth thee.

(DEUTERONOMY 16:20, KJV)

February 8, 1999

Hear our cry, oh Lord, do not grow weary of our complaints! We are not able to bring justice back to our land! There are many people who cry out for justice, but their voices are being stilled. The land is in tumult, as right strives with evil and evil prevails. Unless there arises a person out of the multitude who can resist the forces that govern us, we have no one whom we can follow.

The Holy Spirit has moved across the land. There is a multitude of people who have heard His message and believe in His teachings. They know with an assurance that Jesus is Lord and they want to follow in His holy ways, but the majority of the people mock the Trinity. They do not submit themselves to Him. They spread fear and resentment among those who believe in the Trinity. The land has fallen into darkness as the people who hate God mock that which has been considered righteous and which has been cast aside as illegal!

The law of the land was based on the principles of the Trinity. Now if the evil defy God, they are lifted up, only to spread contention among the people. The people who believed in the laws that were founded on the principles of God are belittled. It is as if God has died! The leaders, who want to elevate mankind and who do not want any Godly laws to hamper them, cruelly lash out against those who live righteously.

Your people do not look for trouble! They cannot allow injustice and wickedness to expand to their families. Yet, the new laws take away their rights! They cannot raise their children as they see fit. Across the whole land, wickedness is being taught to the children. They are being given false concepts that will not help them live a successful life on earth.

When a person is taught a false concept in life, it may take years for them to see the fallacy of that teaching. They may even defend it, even when they know inwardly something isn't right about it. Anyone who would bring them the truth is considered an enemy! How dare anyone test the teachings to see if it is true or not!? The people are to be subject to the words of their leaders, or pay the price for their defiance and rebellion!

He Is True, But People Use What They Want of Jesus and Ignore the Rest!

And Jesus came and spake unto them, saying, All power is given unto me in Heaven and in earth. Go ye therefore, and teach all nations, baptizing them in the name of the Father, and of the Son, and of the Holy Ghost: Teaching them to observe all things whatsoever I have commanded you: and, lo, I am with you always, even unto the end of the world. Amen.

(MATTHEW 28:18–20, KJV)

February 9, 1999

We wait, with expectant heart, desiring to see the whole world saved in the name of Jesus. Our lives move by quickly, and all becomes a blur. There are good times and bad times. Some are filled with hope as we see certain people find Jesus and catch His fire. There are times when people refuse to accept the ways of Jesus, and we feel sorry for them. If we are the sent ones, there certainly are many fields ready for harvest—but few want to be in that harvest!

If the average person would be asked, they would declare that they do believe in Jesus. They would declare how faithful they are unto Him. But they would not take their confessions too seriously, and they would go about doing the same things that they did before. There isn't a reality check between their actions and their confession of faithfulness to Jesus!

Jesus is not just an ordinary person who lived long ago. He is a way of life. He is richer in His intent! He gave of Himself so that all people could share in His bounty. He brings richness of life that one cannot discern unless one has really accepted Him and His holy ways. One cannot declare allegiance to someone and then ignore what they stand for! They must accept the whole concept of Jesus, or they are not actually part of Him.

People give of their money to other people who are associated with Jesus. They feel that they can share their wealth with Jesus in this way. Can they buy souls with their money? They can make knowing Jesus easier if they make places available for others to hear the message of Jesus. Yet, each group will select certain parts of Jesus and they will feel as if they are teaching the true Gospel of Jesus! While they are doing this, they condemn other people who want to spread the Word to many people, just as they have a desire to do.

There have been many visions that certain people have received that make them desire to go forth and teach the ways of Jesus. Many people receive these messages and people learn from those who have received the messages, but there is no guarantee that they understand what is really sent to people from Jesus.

One must know Scripture and the true ways of God to keep walking in the truth of Jesus. He is true, but people use what they want of Jesus and ignore the rest!

WHO AND WHERE
ARE THEY TODAY?

And Jesus looked round about, and saith unto his disciples,
How hardly shall they that have riches enter into the kingdom
of God! And the disciples were astonished at his words. But
Jesus answereth again, and saith unto them, Children, how
hard is it for them that trust in riches to enter into the king-
dom of God!

(MARK 10:23–24, KJV)

February 10, 1999

We give You thanks, Lord Jesus, for drawing us unto You. There are many people we meet daily who don't know You. Many people seem to be happy and content with their lives. They live in fine houses and have good jobs. They have a lovely family and dress well. There is really nothing that they cannot have. If money is the answer, then they have no questions. We live in a very prosperous age!

Those who know Jesus are aware of who they are. They can see a joy that can only come from knowing Jesus. He fills in the empty spaces in a person's life. He lets them know that there is more to life than money. He declares that the way one earns money is important, that there is a payday for living righteously in Him.

There are many Christians who fail to reach the level of success that non-Christians do. They seem to be less prosperous. Is it because money is not as important to them? Each person wants to be comfortable while they live on earth. They see that money buys them many friends. People fear to defy the prosperous because the rich can cause trouble for them. So people go about their daily lives tiptoeing around influential people, to avoid stirring their anger.

Since Christians have a strict moral code of ethics, they can irritate the prosperous because money doesn't come first with believers. Others are angered when Christians can be happy with little. It belies the notion that money can buy happiness in life, so they become an enemy of anyone who appears to have something that they can't buy.

Jesus owned very few things. Yet, everywhere He went, He was welcomed by the people who knew Him. There were times when He slept outside, under the stars. At all times, Jesus had the responsibility of caring for those people who followed after Him. He was concerned for their physical welfare.

In compassion, He would feed those who were following Him. He did not make a practice of it, or He would have drawn all the people after Him only for the things that He could provide for them. It was still necessary for the people to make a living, and then see Jesus when He was nearby.

The leaders could not understand Jesus and His purpose. They did not want change! They liked being rich and important. They wanted the people to follow them and bow before them! Who and where are they today?

It Takes Truly Discerning People to Realize That Something They Are doing Needs Changed

And none considereth in his heart, neither is there knowl-edge nor understanding to say, I have burned part of it in the fire; yea, also I have baked bread upon the coals thereof; I have roasted flesh, and eaten it: and shall I make the residue thereof an abomination? Shall I fall down to the stock of a tree? He feedeth on ashes: a deceived heart hath turned him aside, that he cannot deliver his soul, nor say, Is there not a lie in my right hand?

(ISAIAH 44:19–20, KJV)

February 11, 1999

Let there be glory, honor, and praises unto the Lord Jesus Christ! He is worthy of our praise! In Him is all the goodness that can be found in people. People search the world for honest people. When they find them, do they dote on them and bow before them? No! There is a time of testing and trial, to see if they are really true. It doesn't take too long before they find a weakness in them!

Do they go forth and declare that they have met a person who is much to be obeyed? No! They tell about the flaw that they think they have found. Only a perfect person would recognize another perfect person. Since there is no such person, people who seek perfection will never find it. It will forever be a goal that no one really wants to find. It only makes them more imperfect when they find a person who is above reproach!

Yet, there can be many people who set goals for themselves, and they strive to attain them. When people love Jesus and try to emulate Him, they are searching for a perfect thing. Jesus judges in love, seeing the good that a person has really done. He knows all the weaknesses in people. He is delighted when a man repents and turns away from his sin. This is worthy of man, for he saw that which was unacceptable. First, he knew that Jesus declared that it was wrong. Secondly, he set his heart toward righteousness and determined to do it. He realized that he had a sinful nature in a certain area and he set out to remove it. Well done, my true and faithful servant.

He understood that people are a combination of good and bad. It is up to them to search out that which is good and continue to expand the goodness in life. It takes truly discerning people to realize that something they are doing needs to be changed. To change means that something they are doing is not acceptable to Jesus; to gain insight in the ways of God tells that they are searching for the good that is in them. They are not totally wicked; they will seek that which brings pleasure unto the Father God.

The insight that is found in a person relates to the type of person one really is. Being willing to change means not being satisfied with one's spiritual character, and wanting to change one's life for the better!

SCRIPTURE RELATES THE CAUSES THAT MADE THIS DISTRESS FALL ON THEM

> *Behold, the LORD's hand is not shortened, that it cannot save; neither his ear heavy, that it cannot hear: But your iniquities have separated between you and your God, and your sins have hid his face from you, that he will not hear. For your hands are defiled with blood, and your fingers with iniquity; your lips have spoken lies, your tongue hath muttered perverseness.*
>
> *(ISAIAH 59:1–3, KJV)*

February 12, 1999

There are times when the children of God become weary and heavy-laden by the evil that is happening about them. They love the Lord Jesus Christ, and they want Him to rule over them and their land. All too often, wickedness makes itself known and there is defiance against the Trinity. With great disgust, the children of God let it be known that they are unhappy with the events of the day! They do all that they can to follow the ways of God, but all seems to be futile!

Great distress fell on the Israelites over the years. Scripture relates the causes that made this distress fall on them. The people had separated themselves from God. If the people wanted to follow after wickedness, God wasn't going to do anything about it. They would suffer the consequences of following after other gods.

When they rejected the ways of God, they rejected God Himself. They wanted control of their own destiny, and God let them do as they pleased.

After many warnings sent to the people by the Prophets of God, the land would suffer at the mercy of their neighbors. The Israelites were once strong and had captured many peoples, but when they defied God and honored other gods, they became easy prey to any marauding army that mobilized against them. With much agony and pain, they realized that if they were to remain strong, they needed to return to God. God would forgive them and restore them to power. They would once again become a powerful people. They lived in peace.

Today, the people of America have turned away from God! They have broken His laws that help maintain balance in a land. They rejected that which has guided them through the problems in the past. The people defy the Trinity and laugh at the idea that there is really a Spiritual force that helps rule and govern nations. In defiance of God, they do that which pleases them. They have become more wicked than Israel, when God rejected that nation! Here in America, there are many people who have become closer to God than at any other time in history. Many marvelous deeds are done in the name of Jesus. Miracles take place daily due to the prayers of those Christians who are set upon the ways of the Trinity. But unless the people believe the way that the Trinity works, the Christians are held in contempt by those who refuse to believe. They will not give credit to the Trinity, no matter how strongly the evidence points to the Trinity. The people must suffer as a whole for their rebellion!

We Have No Fears That You Can't Calm

Fear thou not; for I am with thee: be not dismayed; for I am thy God: I will strengthen thee; yea, I will help thee; yea, I will uphold thee with the right hand of my righteousness.

(ISAIAH 41:10, KJV)

February 13, 1999

Jesus be the Lord of all! Jesus, we surrender all! Help us to be all that we should be. Strengthen us daily in all our needs. We have no fears that You can't calm. You are our strength all–day long. The fact is that in You we trust. Blessed Jesus, our All in all!

People can see all the evil and corruption on earth. Their minds can often be repulsed by the horrors they see. Powerless, they watch as if they were not a part of that struggle. They can donate money to their favorite causes, but do they ever know if that, which may seem little to them, has really made a change?

The world and its people have become smaller and smaller. Nations that were once isolated and unafraid of being attacked by anyone are now fearful that they could be destroyed by an unfriendly people. The people of the world get ideas in their minds, and they may decide that which does not belong to them can be theirs by sheer force.

Those traits that once made a people unique are disappearing. The world has communications that allow people in distant lands the ability to see how other people are living. The desire to be there and be like these foreign people rises up in them. Although they do not understand the others' cultures, they see it as being better than their own. They do not know the means, which someone else must supply, to live as they do. There is no Garden of Eden, where everything is given to them free. It is as difficult for these other people to live as it is for them in their own land.

People make their own culture. They are unique in the way that they handle everyday life. It is a credit to our Creator that people have the ability to conquer the land they live in. People should not desire to have things that they cannot control. It can only bring upheaval to them.

When one nation receives a weapon of great destruction, another nation will want the same thing, only better, to protect themselves. Can anyone trust a warlike nation to reserve their weapons for defense only? Or will that nation strike to defeat their hated neighbor before their neighbor has a chance to get their weapon of mass destruction? People would rule the earth, but do they do it wisely?

I Loved Him from My Youth, But I Didn't Know Him

O God, thou hast taught me from my youth: and hitherto have I declared thy wondrous works.

(PSALM 71:17, KJV)

February 15, 1999

Heart of my heart, the Lord Jesus reigns within me in love. He has come to me because I asked Him to come and save me. He came and He changed my whole life. The person that I once was began to look at my soul, and there was ugliness and sin inside. Jesus knew me as a little child and He was with me, but I didn't really know Him. We were two who were searching for a love match, and we finally met each other!

Oh! What joy on my part! For Jesus became real to me. I no longer saw Him as a wonderful person who lived long ago. He became real to me. It didn't matter when I accepted Him in my life. It didn't matter how many sins I had committed before I really met Him. All that mattered was that, through His magnificent power, He took my sins away. He made me a righteous person in the eyes of God.

I loved Him from my youth, but I didn't know Him. He did cleanse me from past sins, but I didn't know His ways. He began to teach me through His Holy Spirit, that which was acceptable moral behavior to Him. Even after I had met Him, remnants of my past sinful nature would rise up in me. He has called me righteous, but there wasn't true righteousness in me. I had to learn the ways of righteousness. That righteousness is found in Scripture. It was written long ago for all people who would seek true righteousness. It was up to me to find what it really was and how to adapt it to my life.

The Holy Spirit, in His own marvelous way, took me as I was and began to remove the layers of sin that were in me. Sometimes it was painful, as I saw the old me disappear and a new me emerge. But the new me gave me peace and joy. There was contentment in knowing that I finally knew the truth of life. I saw life as a wonderful experience, with all its challenges and heartaches.

Then I knew that people are not mindless beings who live on earth for a brief time, to wither away into nothingness. But they are a gift unto Jesus who knew them and loved them before they were born, that His life was given for them, that they could spend eternity together in peace. That righteousness is a blessing in itself, and anyone who is blessed enough will embrace Jesus for an eternity. Life is sweet since I met Jesus! The old me has gone away and I stand anew, ready to meet Jesus eternally!

If People Find Contentment on Earth, They Have Found the Secret of Life

Perverse disputings of men of corrupt minds, and destitute of the truth, supposing that gain is godliness: from such withdraw thyself. But godliness with contentment is great gain. For we brought nothing into this world, and it is certain we can carry nothing out.

(I TIMOTHY 6:5–7, KJV)

February 16, 1999

Come bless the Lord, all ye children of the Lord. Worship and adore Him, bow down before Him. He is worthy of your praise! In Jesus, people can find everything that they need in order to satisfy themselves on earth. Jesus loves those who love Him. He has provided for all their needs. If people find contentment on earth, they have found the secret of life.

All too often, people do not find contentment. They think that riches and glory will bring the satisfaction they need. But no matter how far a person goes in life, there is always something more that they want. There are never enough things to bring them the peace that they need, so they blame other people for their discontent and set about to gather more things to themselves. Their happiness is never guaranteed!

It is true that people need to work to achieve their goals in life. They should try to meet all of their family's needs by themselves. They should set reasonable goals for themselves and not compare themselves with others. Life can be rich and rewarding for them if they do that which they have set as goals for themselves. There will be those people who succeed in an area in which another one can't. It doesn't mean that one is a failure. It only means that somewhere along the way, another person was at the right place at the right time. They had the credentials that someone else needed. They found their place in life and continued to grow in it.

There are those people who always seem to be striving for their place in life. Have they set their standards too high? One must consider where they began and how far they have gone. They should learn to forgive themselves for failing to achieve all that they desired. They should rejoice and be glad that they have life and that there is something to come that can be better than life on earth.

The laws of God are remarkable when people begin to assess their lives. They can look at what God has asked of the people, to see if they have succeeded in following His Word. If they have, there is much glory that awaits them! All of the children of God are promised an equal amount of joy. They will rejoice in the fact that they had succeeded in accomplishing the real reason for life.

Who would strive with a brother or a sister in Heaven? No one! They have lived on earth and fought a good fight. They were accepted by God and now have a place in Heaven. Their life on earth accomplished what God had intended for all of His children!

Eve Knew the Ways of God and of Adam

And Adam called his wife's name Eve; because she was the mother of all living.

(GENESIS 3:20, KJV)

February 17, 1999

Let there be glory, honor, and praises given unto the Lord Jesus Christ! He is worthy of our praise. When we look at the miracle of man, we know that we did not just happen to be. There had to be a superior intellect that created mankind. The very idea of two creatures mating and making more people in their image is marvelous. Only someone who would love His creation would think of such a marvelous plan.

When people failed to live up to the ideals of the Father God, He still cared enough for His creation to find a way they could be redeemed. He loved them far more than they loved Him! One may wonder, do people have the ability to love as God loves? As only a creation of God, were people created equal to God?

God knew these questions would be asked of men, so to prove to the people that a person could be as perfect as God, He sent Jesus. Jesus was born of a woman. She is His human side, with all the characteristics that people have. He did not have any advantage over other people. He was born of a woman and died as a person. No special physical, supernatural abilities were found in His human state.

At the same time, He was created by His Father God. God did not give Him a special, supernatural body. He was capable of death, just like any other person! Jesus had all the feelings and frailties of people. The intellect that God gave to Jesus is another matter. He thought as people think, but he had Spiritual insights that most people do not recognize in themselves. These insights are Spiritually discerned; they come from the Father. Yet, Adam and Eve conversed with God the Father. Did they have special supernatural, Spiritual gifts that people of today do not have? They were made perfect just as Jesus was. They knew God on a personal level. Adam knew the mind of God. Eve, who was drawn from Adam, had many of the abilities of Adam, but she was not as Adam. He was the first man. There was no way that Adam could reproduce after his own kind. Eve, drawn from the body of Adam, was not made as Adam was. She became the mother of all mankind!

Eve knew the ways of God and of Adam. She learned from them the Spiritual graces that God had placed on them. People, when brought into a situation of high intellect, will react in a manner that they see. Eve was earthly. She understood both the ways of God and of maintaining life on earth!

His Life Was an Open Book
for All People to Read

And the Word was made flesh, and dwelt among us, (and
we beheld his glory, the glory as of the only begotten of the
Father,) full of grace and truth.

(JOHN 1:14, KJV)

February 18, 1999

Come bless the Lord, all ye servants of the Lord Jesus Christ. He is powerful and wise. Those people who lift Him up and who seek Him for wisdom will never be discouraged. He is the One who keeps them mentally and Spiritually in the good things in life!

All too often, Jesus is separated from life on earth. Yes, Jesus was a unique person. He had an unusual character. He looked after the people of the earth even before they were born. He showed them how to live on earth so that they would have a successful life here.

Jesus knew the character flaws that people could draw to themselves. He showed them ways to live a peaceful life on earth. He gave them all the information they would need to live a life that was well-pleasing to them. He never demanded they follow Him. He gave them minds that could decide which way they could live their lives. He told them, in story form, how to conquer their problems. He was fair and just. Not only did He live what He preached, He lifted up those people along the way who misunderstood His teachings. His life was an open book for all people to read. He had nothing to be ashamed of.

Still, at His death, He died a painful and, according to the ideas of the people of the time, a shameful death. The death of hanging on a cross until dead was reserved for the most-hardened criminals of the time. There is no proof that Jesus ever broke any laws, but the political rulers of the time presented false accusations against Him. They had determined that Jesus was a fearful enemy of the throne and that, although He had no army, He was worthy of death.

There were many people who loved Him and supported Him. They could have resembled an army to the wicked, fearful leaders of the time. Jesus brought ideas of righteousness and justice. He stirred up the memories of the Israelites so that they remembered their roots. Their past leaders had ruled over many nations and they were known for their valor in battle. An idea can stir up strength in people, and they will fight to the death to support their ideas. The leaders were afraid of the glory of the past!

WE COULD NEVER EXPECT ANYTHING NEW TO HAPPEN IF WE DON'T TRY

And all the city was gathered together at the door. And he healed many that were sick of divers diseases, and cast out many devils; and suffered not the devils to speak, because they knew him. And in the morning, rising up a great while before day, he went out, and departed into a solitary place, and there prayed. And Simon and they that were with him followed after him. And when they had found him, they said unto him, All men seek for thee. And he said unto them, Let us go into the next towns, that I may preach there also: for therefore came I forth.

(MARK 1:33–38, KJV)

February 19, 1999

N o matter what the weather, sunshine or rain, as long as true Christians get together, there is joy, for Jesus has let us know that there is victory in Him! Life has many problems, but people can find a way out of them. The disappointing trial of yesterday has taught us new strengths, and we can face the future in expectation of great things to come!

"But my life isn't very exciting!" one may declare. They are looking at their lives in a bad way. Life can be enjoyed just because one lives! We could never expect anything new to happen if we don't try. There are others who are just waiting for someone to start something that smacks of adventure, so they can take part in it!

The Jewish people had looked for a long time for their Savior. There were many fine people who rose up out of the masses; the Jewish people looked to see if these were the Messiah. Only Jesus proved to be the One. Because there were others who came forward, the truth of Jesus was hidden from many. They were disappointed in those who had come because they did not see the change that they had hoped for in their Messiah.

Jesus came and there were many who believed in Him. Those who believed strongly enough helped carry the message of the Jewish Messiah to all the world. The people whom Jesus chose carried His message to the world. That message has proven to be true throughout the centuries. Any group of people who embrace it and adopt His ways find themselves living in a better society!

When a nation bases its beliefs on those of Jesus, they find that they have a better nation. A better nation, because of its moral values, encourages its people to move forward in confidence. They see life as a good thing, with an afterlife that is to be more excellent than their mortal life on earth.

The message that Jesus gave to humankind is still in force! It works for all who embrace it! It is alive, as if it has a life of its own. It doesn't matter who embraces it; it makes them better people. In each person, a hope of better things to come—and faith in Jesus and their fellow man—makes life richer!

ALL THAT A PERSON DOES
IS PICKED UP AND REFLECTED
ONTO OTHERS

Jesus said unto him, Thou shalt love the Lord thy God with all
thy heart, and with all thy soul, and with all thy mind. This
is the first and great commandment. And the second is like
unto it, Thou shalt love thy neighbour as thyself. On these two
commandments hang all the law and the prophets.

(MATTHEW 22:37–40, KJV)

February 20, 1999

Come and let us go unto the mountain of our God, unto the house of our Lord. He will bless us and cause His face to shine upon us, so that we will know His ways. We will walk in the strength of His knowledge, and life will be glorious for us. When people are assured of the ways of God, they can go forth in power. They know that all that Jesus has said are of value to them. In Jesus, one grows stronger every day. Let us rejoice and be glad.

It is not difficult to give praise to Jesus. He is a light in a dark and wicked world. At this time, the world is being thrown into spiritual darkness. Religion is not the guiding light it once was for the people. In times past, to know the ways of God was to know righteousness. All one needed to do was to read Scripture, determine what it means, and then do it. They were then sure that if they obeyed the Ten Commandments, they would be protected from injustice.

The Ten Commandments are still the best guide a person can have for life on earth. They will find contentment on earth because they will have a feeling of well-being. All the things on earth will be in harmony and peace will abound. It is when people refuse to follow the ways of God that everything gets out of balance. If they see the Ten Commandments as just laws that they can obey or disobey, and they choose to disobey them, they begin to have problems in many areas of their lives.

All of creation was made by God! He orchestrated that which would be necessary to maintain a peaceful life. But when people think that they are better than the law and do as they please, they cannot claim protection from God. God has given the bare minimum of rules for the people to follow. Every day, when certain circumstances arise, people are called upon to make choices. These choices reflect who they really are—their characters!

They have a choice, to choose who they will be! A follower of God who keeps the universe in place or a dissenter who would bring destruction wherever they go. "But the things I do will only hurt me!" they exclaim. This is not true; all that a person does is picked up and reflected onto others. They can be a model person whom people emulate for righteousness, or one who spreads dissent and anger.

It Is During the Times of Solving One's Problems That a Person Gains Integrity

For the people shall dwell in Zion at Jerusalem: thou shalt weep no more: he will be very gracious unto thee at the voice of thy cry; when he shall hear it, he will answer thee. And though the Lord give you the bread of adversity, and the water of affliction, yet shall not thy teachers be removed into a corner any more, but thine eyes shall see thy teachers: And thine ears shall hear a word behind thee, saying, This is the way, walk ye in it, when ye turn to the right hand, and when ye turn to the left.

(ISAIAH 30:19–21, KJV)

February 22, 1999

Blessed Jesus, still our refuge in good times, as well as in bad times. There is a danger at both times for the unprepared soul! When times are good, a person can get carried away with the riches of life. They expect everything to run smoothly. They become spoiled and want to be pampered! It is no longer a case of being treated as special on occasion; it becomes an expectation on the part of that person. They can become haughty and arrogant in their treatment of others, as if they were better than them, that they are so special they have no regard for others.

Still, everyone would say that they would like to be treated in a special way. They would never understand humility. They can't tell the difference between acting like a spoiled person and one who is being treated as they deserve. This is where deception comes in! A person cannot see when their wants have become supercilious and that they have become overbearing in their mannerisms.

Hard times can come to anyone at any time. One can prepare the best way they know how, but they are just pawns in life. If there is a larger agenda than themselves, things can happen that they don't expect! There comes a time when the old ways pass away. That which one's parents had to do when they were alive changes. They move on and life can become difficult when the ideas of people change. There is never a way to go back to the days of one's youth; that life moves, on and all too quickly for most people, becomes more apparent as people grow older. They knew that their parents had times of struggle, but they overcame their challenges and overcame them—quite easily, if one remembers correctly.

Oh, if only one would know the end of a thing before the beginning! Of course, they could walk through adversity without any worry! They could handle the end very well because they have already understood the problem and settled it. It is during the times of solving one's problems that a person gains integrity. They are faced with things that can make a better person out of them! The successful end of a problem gives people confidence in their ability to conquer their problems and appear to be heroes to those who know them!

THEY BEGIN TO FEEL LIFE
IN A NEW WAY

*And whatsoever ye do, do it heartily, as to the Lord, and
not unto men; Knowing that of the Lord ye shall receive the
reward of the inheritance: for ye serve the Lord Christ. But he
that doeth wrong shall receive for the wrong which he hath
done: and there is no respect of persons.*

(COLOSSIANS 3:23–25, KJV)

February 23, 1999

Jesus, be the Lord of all! Jesus, we surrender all! Help us to be
all that You would have us be. Waken us to Your will! Help us
determine Your ways and stick to them. We love You and You have
set us free. We are not slaves who must pay for their master's good
will! We are lovers of our souls, and they have been given freely
unto Jesus, the One who is the Keeper of our souls!

All too often, people accept things that can be harmful to
them. They are promised many good things if they will give money
toward the cause. But once the money is in the hands of the person who is the head of the plan, the donors are cast aside. They
receive little or nothing in return! They have been taken advantage
of by someone who has no regard for them.

The offended party may cry, "Foul, foul!" but it's of no conse-
quence. There is no way that they can afford to collect their money

from the one who received it! They are left destitute and alone, feeling very foolish, indeed!

When a person comes to Jesus Christ, there is a promise given by them that they will serve the Lord Jesus Christ. Immediately, they begin to receive benefits from Jesus. They start to understand the moral matters in life. They begin to feel life in a new way. They are never cheated! They can associate as much or as little as they please with Jesus. The more they worship and obey Him, the more He gives to them. They can never outgive the Lord!

But it isn't money that Jesus desires. Money is of a different culture. There are many places to which a person may give their money for a good cause, but that is up to that person. Jesus doesn't require a monetary price placed upon Him or His works.

Does money affect the Christian? Of course, people live in two spheres. One is God, Jesus, and the Holy Spirit. There, one may receive freely all that They have to give. Money is not to rule their lives. It is to be placed in perspective, about its true value and why it is needed. The other sphere is one where money rules supreme. If one wants the things of the world, then they are required to pay for them!

It Is of Immense Importance That True Justice Prevails!

My flesh trembleth for fear of thee; and I am afraid of thy judgments. I have done judgment and justice: leave me not to mine oppressors. Be surety for thy servant for good: let not the proud oppress me.

(Psalm 119:120–122, KJV)

February 24, 1999

Jesus shall stand while life on earth degenerates before the people. When everything seems to be dark and life loses its purpose for people, Jesus shall rise up as a true hope. There is a spirit in people that really wants righteousness to prevail. They can stand wickedness for a while, but when sin becomes so intense, people will search for a new way to live.

People believe that if they are left alone, they will live a life of contentment. That is true to a certain extent: people will gather together in towns because they need others around them! They find that there is safety in numbers, but it is in the gathering of people together that quarrels arise. That is why there is a tolerance for wickedness on a lower level. They put up with their neighbors' ways even though their neighbors do not think and act as they would like.

So people are torn by their own individual thoughts and actions, and the act of surrounding themselves with others for protection. That is why laws are passed. Laws determine what is acceptable to the majority of the people. It helps people decide what is right or wrong.

There are many people who disregard the law of the land. They have their own agendas for what they do. They get involved with assorted matters, and they desire to do things their way. If they refuse to obey the laws, there needs to be a higher court that is willing to decide who is right or who is wrong.

Does it always matter who is right or who is wrong? It is of immense importance that true justice prevails! When lawbreakers escape punishment, it weakens the fabric of society. It declares that society can't govern itself, that the government is weak and ineffectual, and it cannot settle simple disputes.

People have to decide which way they should live. Either they support their government or it is ineffectual. If it is ineffectual, then they should try another form of government, one that has the wisdom and power to bring true justice to its people!

They Try to Work Around the Laws of God to Get What They Want!

In this was manifested the love of God toward us, because that God sent his only begotten Son into the world, that we might live through him. Herein is love, not that we loved God, but that he loved us, and sent his Son to be the propitiation for our sins. Beloved, if God so loved us, we ought also to love one another.

(I JOHN 4:9–11, KJV)

February 25, 1999

"Say a prayer for me tonight," people ask of others. They just want to know if they can find someone who will stand with them in a moment of disaster. They have little faith in their own prayers. If God was listening to them, He would have never let them get into the trouble that they are having. Maybe some other person is walking in grace and God will miraculously change the situation!

Time and chance happen to everyone. One can never know when something will emerge that can cause them a problem, but it doesn't mean that Jesus has turned His back on them! Often, they don't really know Jesus and what He is really like. They may never have asked Him into their lives. They may think that they are His, but they really don't pay much attention to what Jesus is all

97

about. They have never taken on His true character, and so they don't know how they are required to act.

Any time is a time to learn about Jesus and His goodness! A person should understand what Jesus is all about! Is He a foolish, suffering man who went to His death expecting the people of the world to follow Him because He loved them more than they loved Him? Jesus knew the frailties of the people, and He stood in their place before God! God is the only One who could bring people into a position where they could find the better things in life. Within themselves, people are not able to redeem themselves. They did not place themselves in a sinful position—that was done for them. They suffered because one man made a pact with evil. They inherited that burden!

Did time and chance have anything to do with Adam's sin? No! He knew God, he knew what he was doing when he turned away from God and disobeyed Him. It was not a gamble on Adam's part. He openly rebelled against God.

Can people today claim to be any better than Adam? Do they know right from wrong? Should they whine when time and chance come against them? They want the blessings of Jesus, but they refuse to pay the price! They try to work around the laws of God to get what they want. When problems arise, they seek someone who has an "in" with God. Yet, in Jesus they already have an "in." All they have to do is look to Jesus and believe in Him!

Adam and Eve Were Striving for Their Own Authority Even though They Didn't Have a Need!

For Adam was first formed, then Eve. And Adam was not deceived, but the woman being deceived was in the transgression. Notwithstanding she shall be saved in childbearing, if they continue in faith and charity and holiness with sobriety.

(I TIMOTHY 2:13–15, KJV)

February 26, 1999

Let there be glory, honor, and praise unto the Lord Jesus Christ! Worship and adore Him. He has true love for the people of earth. There is no greater love than one person may give His life for others. Jesus, seeing the deplorable situation of His Creation, decided to come to earth as a man and give His life for them.

In the beginning, Adam and then Eve had personal contact with God. They were exalted beings because they saw God and they had a close relationship with Him. Their minds were turned toward God and they delighted in His presence. They were truly the children of God. Their thoughts were as one! That which the Father thought, they understood and could follow the way He spoke to them.

There came a time when a serpent brought other ideas. Adam and Eve had never heard different opinions before. When they heard other ideas that made them feel equal with God, and that God had restrained them from thinking their own thoughts, they rebelled against God.

They truly loved God and thought that they would not be in any danger. For He had made them. He loved them. He would tolerate their disobedience to Him. They were wrong! The thoughts of a person make up who they are. If they rebelled against God, there would always be a controversy on matters of importance. God could not lie, nor did He intend to allow rebellion in His Paradise. He loved Adam and Eve, and because of this great love, He did not want to see them destroy the perfection of His perfect land.

If Adam and Eve had found a better way to live, then God allowed them to work out their desires. He knew that life in Paradise was as good as life could get. Adam and Eve were striving for their own authority even though they didn't have a need. God never acted arrogantly toward them. He never belittled them. He taught them great secrets. They were not capable of understanding the character needed to rule over others in wisdom.

They lost their insight into God, and what it means to walk and talk with God. To be a companion of God's takes daily conversations with Him. When it comes to judging a situation, the way of Jesus is always right. To argue with the precedents that have been given to people only leads to further separation from the Trinity!

WHEN ABSOLUTE TRUTH HAS COME, WHO WOULD SEARCH FOR A LESSER BELIEF?

Now the God of patience and consolation grant you to be likeminded one toward another according to Christ Jesus: That ye may with one mind and one mouth glorify God, even the Father of our Lord Jesus Christ. Wherefore receive ye one another, as Christ also received us to the glory of God.

(ROMANS 15:5–7, KJV)

February 27, 1999

Come bless the Lord, all ye children of the Lord! As Jesus is, so shall those who believe in Him become. They will be as One. Just like the Trinity are One, so shall they be. They will be separate, yet their Spirit shall be as one. Each working toward the same goal, each believing the same thing, each adamant in their belief!

When absolute truth has come, who would search for a lesser belief? If people have trusted Jesus to be their salvation, if they expect the Holy Spirit to teach them the wisdom of God, if they trust God to be the true God who created all, then they will be as One.

People have searched earth for the peaceful kingdom where everyone is in one accordance with all that one does. There are no two people who believe exactly the same about anything! They

101

have disagreements on almost everything! Since people are individuals, they process things in their minds, and then add them to the circumstances that they have experienced in life. They come to a certain conclusion! No one else can access these happenings in exactly the same way. Each person is different.

But people can be a witness to the same situation and can corroborate someone else's testimony. They can agree on what is happening before them. They can enter it into their minds the way that they have seen and understood it. Their end result may be different but their testimony is true! Those who believe in Jesus Christ will be of one mind concerning Him. They will tell their story about the way they met Jesus and received His wonderful salvation. They will know that He has changed them for the better. He will bring them peace of mind.

At the same time, they will be more opinionated about righteousness. They will search for true justice. They will love the Trinity more, and they will know Their way. It will not be exactly the same way that someone else has been brought to an understanding of the work of Jesus, but it will still bring them to the throne of Judgment, where they shall be made as one with the Trinity. Or they will be rejected, because all their life will be brought to the throne room, and there they will be judged by the way they did the job that they were given to do!

I Want to Have Fun and Own Rich and Expensive Things!

Charge them that are rich in this world, that they be not high-minded, nor trust in uncertain riches, but in the living God, who giveth us richly all things to enjoy; That they do good, that they be rich in good works, ready to distribute, willing to communicate;

(I Timothy 6:17–18, KJV)

March 1, 1999

My whole being rejoices in Jesus my Savior! He washes all my troubles away. He helps me see beyond today and into the goodness of tomorrow! No fear can encompass me because He has assured me that which is to come is sufficient for me.

Because people are sinful and weak, they make themselves miserable. They have a desire for something. When they get it, they want something else. They will strive for that which they think they need. They have few scruples when it comes to acquiring those things that they earnestly desire at the time.

If they would assess the matter honestly, they would find that it isn't really necessary for them to have that which they recently desired. It was a passion of the time, but it quickly loses its importance once they have received it.

Jesus wants His people to feel satisfaction with life. He wants them to know the beauty of simple living, where the people put

103

energy into seeking Him instead of things! He is sufficient and fulfilling for them.

"It is not the same!" someone will exclaim. "For me to be happy, I must be able to fulfill all my desires! It isn't any fun to walk across the face of the earth laboring daily for my needs! I want more than needs! I want to have fun and own rich and expensive things! Life is good when I look good. I don't want to deprive myself of anything that appeals to me. I'm of the earth! The earthly part of me has many desires, and depriving myself of them constrains me and makes me feel poor and unworthy!"

There are many people who write about the riches that knowing Jesus can bring. They still know that they are of the world even if they serve Jesus. It is the way thWat they achieve the things they need. There are true "needs" in society that one must face! There is a fine line between needing something and striving to achieve the latest fad and own the newest thing. When purchasing something, one should assess their true need and buy that which fills their need. They are not to buy something that doesn't fulfill their need just to be able to say that they own one.

Things are not bad in themselves. It is the quest for ownership that drives people to get something that is of no use to them!

Both Would Suffer Inwardly
because of the Fight!

Train up a child in the way he should go: and when he is old, he will not depart from it.

(PROVERBS 22:6, KJV)

March 2, 1999

Jesus is the rock of my salvation! His banner over us is love! Love! Many people speak of love in a yearning manner! It is as if love is a hard thing to receive from someone. They see love as a rare commodity, which only a few can find in their lives on earth.

Are they expecting too much of other people? Is there true love inside them? Do they need to devote themselves to someone full time before they are willing to accept anyone's love?

A mother will have a child. She devotes much of her time to that child. Although she trains the child in the best way possible, there are times when that child disagrees with her. When that happens, is a mother supposed to show love to that child? Does she show that love by giving in to that child's every demand? Of course not! The mother is the adult! She should know what is best for her child! She must let the child know that life does have restrictions, and that when a child breaks those restrictions, they place themselves in some type of danger.

A mother can become angry with her children, but she still

loves them and lets them know. Although she is angry and disappointed in her child, she still loves the child, and life can be rich and good for both of them.

There will come a time when a true battle comes, testing the love of the mother and the child. Each of them has determined that they are right. If one is stubbornly trying to prove control over the other, they both know the injustice in their hearts. Love flies away as the two become enemies to each other.

This is the time when the training of the child shows forth. If the mother has taught the child to be fair and caring, there is room for negotiation. If the mother, in times past, has ruled with an iron hand, the child is just openly rebelling against years of tyranny. Love can be strained to the breaking point, where neither mother nor child will take the extra step to make reconciliation between them.

Both would suffer inwardly because of the fight. Each would declare themselves the better of the two. They would demean the other person to their friends, just to prove that they are right. Both have suffered a great loss.

GOD HAS GREAT RESPECT FOR THE TORMENT THAT JESUS SUFFERED ON BEHALF OF MANKIND

When Mordecai perceived all that was done, Mordecai rent his clothes, and put on sackcloth with ashes, and went out into the midst of the city, and cried with a loud and a bitter cry; And came even before the king's gate: for none might enter into the king's gate clothed with sackcloth. And in every province, whithersoever the king's commandment and his decree came, there was great mourning among the Jews, and fasting, and weeping, and wailing; and many lay in sackcloth and ashes.

(ESTHER 4:1–3, KJV)

March 3, 1999

You make my heart laugh and cause my heart to sing! You fill my life with joy and now the praises ring! You are Lord and there is no one above You. You and the Father are One, the Holy Spirit dwells within You, and He teaches us the true meaning of life. We can enjoy life because that is the way that God had planned for people to be.

One cannot deny it, but there are many hard times that mankind faces. They run after the Trinity, crying, "Help me, help me!" But people do their own thing, and when trouble arises, they put on sackcloth and ashes and become pious, ready to serve God!

"Has not Scripture said that if we believe in Jesus, all good things will come unto me?" Yet they fail to understand that God is a covenant-type God, who has great respect for the torment that Jesus suffered on behalf of mankind. When one enters into battle, the fiercer the battle, the longer a person remembers the horror of it. They will take the memory of that time with them to the grave!

"It was the best of times, it was the worst of times..." Indeed, while one is going through these times, they have little else they can think about. Their whole being is placed on that problem. They have little energy for anything else! They put everything that they have into winning their struggle. That they remain alive to be able to tell about it is a testimony to the strength and courage that they displayed while they went through that horrible time.

"Victory!" they exclaim. "I have met the enemy and I have triumphed over them!" Yet, deep inside of that person, there is a battle that rages. They may relive one or more parts of that battle many times. They may recall those people who stood beside them, sharing those times. Just to talk to them once again reassures them that it was one of the most horrifying times of their lives also.

"Why the best of times?" one would ask. "No one faces danger or death without some thought about their own safety and the consequences that comes with them!" Some battles are bigger than life. If one has the duty to have this great adventure, then they take it upon themselves to do that which they think is right, a good cause, for much is expected of them!

THEY TREAT OTHERS LIKE THEY WANT TO BE TREATED

Neither was there any among them that lacked: for as many
as were possessors of lands or houses sold them, and brought
the prices of the things that were sold, And laid them down at
the apostles' feet: and distribution was made unto every man
according as he had need.

(ACTS 4:34–35, KJV)

March 4, 1999

We will sing of our Redeemer! On the cross, He died for me! He is mine, yet not me alone, but everyone who comes unto Him will receive of Him. Just like people who live on earth, those who search for the good things in life will be able to find them in Jesus Christ. He has given of the riches of the earth to mankind, and those who seek after them diligently will find them.

Jesus has not declared that riches will help buy a person a place of honor in Heaven. All who seek Him will be judged by the purity of their soul. One may be rich or poor, yet there is a place of honor for all who seek Jesus and the truth.

Inside each person is the ability to be acceptable to Jesus. Jesus has not set standards that can be bought with money. The character of a person can be nurtured in a loving home that understands what Jesus teaches. His ways have never changed, and they are as effective today as they were when Jesus was preparing them for those who would emulate and follow after Him.

Simple! The ways of Jesus are so simple. People only need to have regard and respect for other people, that they treat others like they want to be treated. They are helpful in a time of need. They do not take advantage of others when they are in a tight spot and are forced to take that which comes along. They lift up others when they have had tragedy. They respect those who are trying to lead a righteous life.

It seems as if all these are wonderful, and that everyone would take part in doing these. It all depends upon the person and the opportunity that presents itself. Some people believe that God helps those who help themselves, even if it is taking advantage of a stranger. Money should not be the only reason why someone helps others.

There was a need to support the Christians in the early Church. The reason the Christians in Jerusalem were so poor was that they sold their properties and retained no assets to support themselves. Soon, there were many people who wanted to live off the charity of other people. This led to poverty and a loss of respect by unbelievers, who saw them as unwise stewards of their goods.

It Is Well to Remember That Death Can Be Only a Breath Away

For he knoweth our frame; he remembereth that we are dust.
As for man, his days are as grass: as a flower of the field, so
he flourisheth. For the wind passeth over it, and it is gone;
and the place thereof shall know it no more.

(PSALM 103:14–16, KJV)

March 5, 1999

Blessed Jesus, still our refuge in sickness and in sorrow! These things are common to mankind. They are made to last for a brief time on earth, and then they pass away. They are like flowers that bloom, displaying all their beauty and grace to all who see them. They steal our hearts and then, all too quickly, fade away from view. They can be remembered because of their fragrance and beauty, but they are much too frail for those who love them!

To others who have known them, leaders and common people alike rise up and are considered to be necessary. For those who have learned to love and trust them, life on earth would be dissolute without them. Regretfully, these people have passed away and life must go on without them.

It is true that while people live they can sin and other people find fault with them. As long as they breathe, they are subject to criticism. But when they die, even those who once were their enemy will declare how wonderful they were. They will remember the good things about them. They will declare that life was richer because that person lived!

It is well to remember that death can be only a breath away, and that a kindness shown to anyone helps others feel better about themselves. It is easy to second-guess the actions of others and to be critical about them. One never really knows the end of a matter in the beginning of a problem. They can only call on their past experiences and try to choose wisely the way that they go.

How does one pray for those people who are openly critical of our decisions? Just like we would like to be prayed for when we make a decision that turns out badly for us. We would always be right! We would be considered a wise and good person, yet we have our own mental system that programs us to figure out problems in a unique way. Let us all be of a sound mind and a gentle heart that is quick to forgive others' mistakes, and encourage others to go forward, trying to be all that they can be.

Let us forgive ourselves, but not delude ourselves that we are perfect. We can test our own hearts and minds to see if our intentions are pure before God. We can pray that righteousness is done, that we may all be saved.

THEY HAVE ONLY ONCE TO LIVE AND THEN THEY MUST EXIST WITH THAT WHICH THEY HAVE GATHERED FOR THEMSELVES ETERNALLY!

And I saw a great white throne, and him that sat on it, from whose face the earth and the Heaven fled away; and there was found no place for them. And I saw the dead, small and great, stand before God; and the books were opened: and another book was opened, which is the book of life: and the dead were judged out of those things which were written in the books, according to their works. And the sea gave up the dead which were in it; and death and hell delivered up the dead which were in them: and they were judged every man according to their works.

(REVELATION 20:11–13, KJV)

March 6, 1999

Let us rejoice and be glad, and give all our glory unto Him, Our Lord Jesus Christ! He has known us at the very beginning, and knew that we would worship and adore Him throughout eternity. We are not scheduled to die like all other living things and be buried in the ground, never to be known again. We are to rise and be with Him! He has made us eternal, and no matter what one's physical body may do, their Spirit will be with Jesus for all eternity.

How do people look at their lives on earth? They would say

that there were good times and bad times. Yet, through all times, Jesus was there to encourage them and guide them to Him. The righteousness of Jesus was imparted in them, and they are better people because of it. How sad that people have become discouraged from finding Jesus.

Jesus has been there for all to see and know. He has encouraged people in all generations to seek Him. He only asks to be their Savior, because He is a vital part of people's lives. People can get so tied up in the physical world that they put the spiritual world away from their thoughts. They work industriously for their material things. They see prosperity as the measure of their worth. When they die and pass on to the spiritual realm, they find that they have failed to lay up riches in Heaven that would last them throughout eternity.

These people cannot come back to change this situation. They have only once to live, and then they must exist with that which they have gathered for themselves eternally. "Oh! If I had only known!" they will moan, as they search diligently to see if any of their good deeds were missed. But their account will be accurate. They have compiled it by themselves. Everything that they have done will be laid before them, unabridged; no one will be there who will look into a matter for them.

In the earthly world, everyone would hope that they can change something that turned out badly for them. They will turn unrighteousness into righteousness, but even if people turn around their evilness and call it "good," it will not appear that way in their own personal book of life.

HE HAS SENT A BLUEPRINT FOR EVERYONE TO SEE

A double minded man is unstable in all his ways.

(JAMES 1:8, KJV)

March 8, 1999

Let us sing of our Redeemer, on the cross He died for me! He sealed my pardon and set me free, freedom from sin and the bondage of sin. All too often, people think that they are free. They can do anything they want to do. They think that if they accept Jesus into their hearts, their freedom to choose between right and wrong will change!

Even though they would like to think that they do not sin to excess, they still want the freedom to do so. If they accept Jesus into their hearts, their right to choose will be gone. They will somehow be forced to be good. One would declare that this is utter nonsense! One should always choose that which is right and not be interested in sin.

This thinking is double minded. Each person, in conversations with other people, declares righteousness. They would have everyone know that they are righteous, and that they know right from wrong. But for them to fear Jesus because they are more likely to become a righteous person against their will is deceit and double mindedness!

115

When a person sets out to do something, they want to do the best possible thing that they can. They don't declare that this is what they want and then work toward another goal. They will move forward, doing the best they know how to do. They will not settle until they achieve their goals.

So when a person declares that they want righteousness, they must sell out to righteousness. Jesus gives people a higher moral sense about matters. He has already set the standard for righteousness. He has sent a blueprint for everyone to see. They are able to meet these standards! Jesus created mankind; He knows their abilities. They can be supernaturally endowed with strength to do that which Jesus has set forth as a standard.

People can set standards that Jesus has not set for them. When they do this, they are placing themselves in jeopardy. They are making themselves a target for others to see if they can abide by the rules they have set for themselves. If their standards are unrealistic, then they will struggle to attain their goals. They are setting themselves up for failure! They are placing their ideas of righteousness above the standard that Jesus has set for mankind! It is wise to understand the ways of Jesus so one may follow them in an even manner.

HE IS TO COME AND RULE OVER
THOSE PEOPLE WHO REMAIN

*The Revelation of Jesus Christ, which God gave unto him, to
shew unto his servants things which must shortly come to
pass; and he sent and signified it by his angel unto his servant
John: Who bare record of the Word of God, and of the testimony of Jesus Christ, and of all things that he saw. Blessed is
he that readeth, and they that hear the words of this proph-
ecy, and keep those things which are written therein: for the
time is at hand.*

(REVELATION 1:1–3, KJV)

March 9, 1999

He is the King of kings and the Lord of lords. He knows the end
before the beginning. All that is to come has been foretold
to those who have an ear to hear and a way to discern the times.
There have been many crises that have destroyed many people at
certain times. Many lost their lives, but those who escaped have
rebuilt civilization.

Jesus has declared that there would be a time when people
would not be able to escape, like they did in times past. He is to
come and rule over those people who remain. There will be those
who will escape the crises of the time.

The time will come when there will be waves of people who will
be protected by Jesus. They are to have information about how to

escape the brunt of the crises by just knowing the information that Jesus has prepared for them. They are to be constant in prayer and have an ear to hear that which will give them the protection they will need!

Not everyone who loves Jesus will escape with their lives. There will be places and times when these good souls will be sacrificed because time and chance have come upon them. Jesus will not sacrifice the souls just because they have missed the message that He has sent to His believers. They will be cared for by Jesus until the time comes when all His people will be gathered together.

Even some of the wicked will escape that which will come upon the earth suddenly. They will answer to Jesus and be punished in a way that they deserve. Wickedness can fall upon the just and the unjust at the same time. It will be determined by the Lord at the end of times, as people know it. There will be a distinction between those who have trusted in Jesus and those who have rejected Him. Trust in Jesus brings a comfort and a knowledge that everything that matters will be cared for by Jesus. He has not brought people to a time such as this to destroy His handiwork.

People would that everyone live a good and peaceful life, that no danger would be able to befall them; that Jesus shall supernaturally rise them up above the fray. But one should not let their future be decided by time and chance if they have the ability to prepare for that which is to come!

JESUS DECLARES THAT PEOPLE ARE TO HAVE HIS SPIRIT

For John truly baptized with water; but ye shall be baptized with the Holy Ghost not many days hence. When they therefore were come together, they asked of him, saying, Lord, wilt thou at this time restore again the kingdom to Israel? And he said unto them, It is not for you to know the times or the seasons, which the Father hath put in his own power. But ye shall receive power, after that the Holy Ghost is come upon you: and ye shall be witnesses unto me both in Jerusalem, and in all Judaea, and in Samaria, and unto the uttermost part of the earth. And when he had spoken these things, while they beheld, he was taken up; and a cloud received him out of their sight. And while they looked stedfastly toward Heaven as he went up, behold, two men stood by them in white apparel;

(ACTS 1:5–10, KJV)

March 10, 1999

We do love You, dear Jesus. You have let us know that all people can be in Your family! We may call You Brother! Yet, You are a King, Lord, Savior, and the only true Son of God! You have said that all that You have can be ours! We are looked upon with favor, and we shall be embraced by You for eternity!

The people of earth, who have gotten to know You, bow down before You! They are so appreciative of all that You have done for them; they do not consider it demeaning. They are aware of the

119

goodness that You bring to them. They know that You are fair and just!

People look for these same traits in one another, but they often fail to find what they search for. "People made in the image of God?" they query. Only Jesus had remained steadfast throughout the years! He has never failed those people who have trusted in Him. He has been there, supporting those people with good intentions toward Him and their fellow Mankind! It is only by knowing Jesus that people know what to expect by looking at others. It is easy to tell if they know Jesus, or if they follow after the ways of the people of earth.

Jesus declares that people are to have His Spirit, that precious Spirit that we call Holy. He is the activator of Jesus who can be in us. As They work together to activate the Spirit who can be a part of us, we must be open to Them and follow in Their ways. In that way, the Spiritual person in us can lead us away from our fleshly desires to a more perfect demeanor before God. We can make our bodies become more God-like daily. We can change the way we understand matters and follow closely the teachings that we have been given.

All change can be difficult! Life can blow people about so that they feel battered and bruised. People cannot always control their future. They are subject to the actions of other people. They can suffer because other people reject Jesus and His ways. But each time someone places away the flesh and looks to Jesus for help, they grow in a Spiritual way. They are more able to put away the body of flesh and take upon themselves the nature of Jesus. It is Jesus who made this possible for them. He has seen to it that people are able to receive His Spirit and walk in a Spiritual way.

THE SWEEPING OF THE
HOLY SPIRIT ENHANCES

And when the day of Pentecost was fully come, they were all with one accord in one place. And suddenly there came a sound from Heaven as of a rushing mighty wind, and it filled all the house where they were sitting. And there appeared unto them cloven tongues like as of fire, and it sat upon each of them. And they were all filled with the Holy Ghost, and began to speak with other tongues, as the Spirit gave them utterance.

(ACTS 2:1–4, KJV)

March 11, 1999

Since Jesus came into my heart, wondrous things have happened! He works with me to bring the best out in me. He blesses me daily with His mercy and grace. He teaches me the good things that I should know, so that life on earth will be sweet, not bitter. To live at a time such as this is to take part in the glory that God has always had for humankind!

There have been many times since the death and resurrection of Jesus Christ that the Holy Spirit has swept across the lands. There have been awakenings in many parts of the world at various times. There has been a prolonged one recently as the Holy Spirit has awakened a nation, already declared to be a Christian nation, with the blessings of God!

These awakenings have not been national in their stirrings. There are many people who do not understand what is taking place all around them. They hear that something wonderful is taking place, but since they feel that they are already Christians who belong to a specific church, there is nothing more to receive from God. But they are in error! The sweeping of the Holy Spirit enhances their belief in God, Jesus, and the Holy Spirit. They begin to receive insights from Them, and they are amazed at how real the Trinity can be; that They are alive and They rule and guide people in paths of righteousness.

There aren't a select few that can be blessed by these things. Anyone who will open themselves up to divine guidance can receive blessings from the Trinity. They are given gifts that are Spiritually discerned, that work in their lives for their benefits. They become more righteous than they have ever been in their lives. They are more able to cope with their troubles in the world. They understand the true Trinity and they know that they are touched by Them daily.

Thank all You again, oh Blessed Trinity, for allowing me to be born at a time such as this. Thank You for letting the poorest to the richest person have the chance to take part in this mighty revival. We see clearly now what the intentions of God have been toward humankind, and we rejoice that this has come about at this time.

Just Like Two People Who Are Getting Married, He Declares That He Loves the Woman

Let us be glad and rejoice, and give honour to him: for the marriage of the Lamb is come, and his wife hath made herself ready. And to her was granted that she should be arrayed in fine linen, clean and white: for the fine linen is the righteousness of saints. And he saith unto me, Write, Blessed are they which are called unto the marriage supper of the Lamb. And he saith unto me, These are the true sayings of God.

(REVELATION 19:7–9, KJV)

March 12, 1999

Blessed assurance, Jesus is mine! He has declared His intentions to the people on earth. He is honest and true, and He will stand by the words that He has given to all mankind. If they will hear Him and do that which He asks of them, they will share in His glory. He does not ask for our lives in return, yet those who know Him freely give of themselves. Wherever He leads them, they shall go!

He fills them with righteousness and love. He asks nothing of them that He is not willing to do. He has given the ultimate sacrifice. He knew that people tended toward unrighteousness. Jesus had to find a way to help them gain strength of purpose in life. So

He discussed it with the Father, who knew what it would take to free the people from their bondages on earth.

A sacrifice so awesome that no one could deny that it was sent from God! Jesus, Himself, the Son of God, gave up His earthly life so that all people, when they died, could join Him in His eternal Kingdom. They could be forgiven for all things through Jesus, who was already made perfect before God. If we are His brothers and sisters, then He, through His sacrifice, could bring salvation to those who declare their intentions to Him.

Just like two people who are getting married, He declares that He loves the woman. She, in turn, promises to love and obey Him. They both sign a marriage pledge that they shall be faithful to each other, until death do them part!

This type of pledge is of value as long as each person fulfills the promise to the other. If one of them sees the pledge broken, they may part and each may go their own way. This comes about with much heartache and pain. One can't make a promise to love, honor, and obey and then take it as worthless. Once it was of value to them, they would never think of separating from the other. Their word was their bond and they did not take it lightly.

Jesus has offered to everyone who will accept His proposal. They are to love, honor, and obey Him; He will never leave them unless they decide to break their pledge. Everlasting life in perfection is a beautiful promise! Who would give that up for anything that the earth has to offer?

THE BLOOD OF JESUS ACTS AS A COVERING AND JESUS CLAIMS THEM AS HIS OWN

If we say that we have fellowship with him, and walk in darkness, we lie, and do not the truth: But if we walk in the light, as he is in the light, we have fellowship one with another, and the blood of Jesus Christ his Son cleanseth us from all sin. If we say that we have no sin, we deceive ourselves, and the truth is not in us.

(I JOHN 1:6–8, KJV)

March 13, 1999

Let us sing of our Redeemer! On the cross, He died for me! He sealed my pardon and set me free. Once I was bound by the law. The law is good in the sense it teaches that which is right and that which is wrong. One may rejoice when they know that they are doing that which is acceptable, or if they are accused of wrongdoing, they can be judged by their peers. They can be declared innocent when they prove that they have not broken a law.

When Jesus died on the cross for the wickedness of mankind, He did not make laws wrong. He gave people the strength to overcome wickedness. They no longer were bound by sin that made law a necessity to govern the people. The law will always be needed; it is the only way that people can decide if they are breaking the statutes or trespassing against the rights of others.

125

People would struggle in the flesh. They wanted to do certain things, but the law declared that it was wrong to do so. Wickedness would make people do those things that they were sorry about after they did them. If they got away with a wicked act, they would be condemned in their hearts and minds. If the wicked act caused trouble for others, they would be tormented because their conscience would not let them rest. They could be tormented by their sinfulness.

Jesus, through His mercy and grace, has allowed truly repentant people to feel the freedom that true forgiveness can bring. Jesus made people acceptable to God by His giving of Himself as a sacrifice for people's sins. Yet, one is not to take this act of goodness lightly. God doesn't see it as a simple thing to allow His own Son to be sacrificed for others' sins. Willful sin is heinous to God. Jesus was God's only begotten Son. Who would dare make a king's son suffer because of their wickedness? People would not tolerate such an act, and neither does God!

People do sin; they may do so by not recognizing what they are doing as sin. They have the ability to come to God for forgiveness when they repent from that sin. The blood of Jesus acts as a covering, and Jesus claims them as His own. God forgives them and they are acceptable to Him; they can live eternally with Him. They have now gained the knowledge and strength to overcome that sin. They go and sin no more! Jesus has made it so that people, even though they sin, can find forgiveness through Jesus.

EACH OF US MUST LOOK AT GUILT WITHOUT A BIASED EYE

Blessed is the man that endureth temptation: for when he is tried, he shall receive the crown of life, which the Lord hath promised to them that love him. Let no man say when he is tempted, I am tempted of God: for God cannot be tempted with evil, neither tempteth he any man: But every man is tempted, when he is drawn away of his own lust, and enticed. Then when lust hath conceived, it bringeth forth sin: and sin, when it is finished, bringeth forth death.

(*JAMES 1:12–15, KJV*)

March 15, 1999

Hear my cry, oh Lord, attend to my prayer. Let true justice spread across this country. Those of us who have gotten to know the values of the Bible are angry and humiliated by the actions of the people who behave unjustly. We know that people are aware of righteousness, because they demand it from those people who are in authority. But they look away from righteousness when they may profit from injustice!

There are those people who condemn others because they have broken some law, yet they look the other way when they see someone whom they like breaking a law! They feel that some law-breaking can be justifiable, as long as they profit from it. Any time they are called guilty of breaking a law, they declare that they are innocent because of who they are, not by what they have done.

Because of these double-minded feelings, true justice cannot be done. They do not look at lawbreaking as being detrimental to anyone. They cannot see the law as being equal. There has to be a reason why someone is caught breaking the law, other than the fact that they are actually guilty. The most violent offender can be excused by some others because of the excuses that are trumped up by people who, for some reason, have a bias.

Each of us must look at guilt without a biased eye. Judgment must be based on what has happened, by the evidence, not by an individual's feelings! So many people would rather be considered a victim than admit they have done wrong. They even lie to themselves, covering up what they have done by excusing it away.

What is really sad is when they leave God and His true justice out of the picture. They pick and choose what they think. They may be on one side one day, and on the exact opposite side the next! They need just a few pieces of information before they make up their minds. They never bother to look at the crime that has been committed to understand whether someone is guilty or not.

People can be swayed by another's attitudes instead of discerning the truth of a matter. If one is to be true, they must seek the truth at its most basic level, then they will truly be seeking justice for all.

THERE IS AN OMINOUS FEELING AS ONE'S PROBLEMS BEGIN TO BUILD

But they and our fathers dealt proudly, and hardened their necks, and hearkened not to thy commandments, And refused to obey, neither were mindful of thy wonders that thou didst among them; but hardened their necks, and in their rebellion appointed a captain to return to their bondage: but thou art a God ready to pardon, gracious and merciful, slow to anger, and of great kindness, and forsookest them not. Yea, when they had made them a molten calf, and said, This is thy God that brought thee up out of Egypt, and had wrought great provocations;

(NEHEMIAH 9:16–18, KJV)

March 16, 1999

I will sing of my Redeemer, on the cross He died for me! He sealed my pardon and set me free! Now, I rejoice in Jesus, for I was a slave to sin. Those things I would not do because they seemed evil to me, could tempt me, and draw me away from righteousness. Now, I can resist evil and do that which is pleasing to God and to myself.

It is a horrible feeling to know that one is defying God because of rebellion against Him. When He has declared that certain things are evil, He already knows the nature of people, and that they could be hurt if they continued on their evil course.

129

People are drawn to sin! It seems to be the only choice they have sometimes. They want to have something, but there is no way that they can attain it in righteousness. They feel as if their lives would be better if they could only get the thing they want. So they will strive to receive the things, which God warns them ahead of time, will cause them trouble. Does it matter to them that they are causing trouble for themselves? When God declares there will be a penalty that they will pay if they persist in getting that which is wrong for them, they will suffer for it.

By persistence, they may be able to get that which is so stridently desired. The taste of accomplishment is sweet, only to find out as time goes by that it has made them more miserable than they were before. There is an ominous feeling as one's problems begin to build. They feel set aside, as that which once was so precious to them loses its value. They will strive for years to rectify that which they had so ardently sought, only to find that there is no true value in something that wasn't right from the beginning.

Listening to God and the wisdom, knowledge, and understanding that He has left to the people of earth will always bring a prudent life. Rebelling, because of lust or any other feeling that one receives during one's lifetime, can only bring heartaches and troubles to them. The guidelines are set before people to follow. They are not set because God likes to control people. They are set so that people can enjoy a richer, fuller life.

Jesus Is a Necessity at Any Age of One's Life

Be careful for nothing; but in every thing by prayer and supplication with thanksgiving let your requests be made known unto God. And the peace of God, which passeth all understanding, shall keep your hearts and minds through Christ Jesus. Finally, brethren, whatsoever things are true, whatsoever things are honest, whatsoever things are just, whatsoever things are pure, whatsoever things are lovely, whatsoever things are of good report; if there be any virtue, and if there be any praise, think on these things.

(PHILIPPIANS 4:6–8, KJV)

March 17, 1999

Blessed Jesus, still our refuge at all times in our lives! As little children, we heard the name of Jesus at our parents' knees. We didn't understand the full meaning of Christ then. We will go to our deaths still searching out His glory! He is so marvelous, and His scope so diversified that there is always some new facet that we can find out about Him.

Those who discovered Jesus at an early age have an advantage in life. They can draw strength from Him as they grow. Jesus is a necessity at any age of one's life. He helps people understand that which is perfect, and that they have been made capable by taking part in grace.

131

Over the years, the people can grow into a closer walk with Jesus. They think as a child when they are small. As they grow older, they see how the Word of God expands to include all their experiences in life. Just as Jesus appears to us first as a baby, we accept His first steps into our lives as children. He is no more to us than some other hero we have read about in other books. But the story of Jesus is power, one that reaches beyond the grave.

People's heroes may die in a valiant battle, but Jesus survives past death. His greatest battle was with death, and He has proven that life continues past one's timeline on Earth. His power remains intact, and His words surpass any language barrier that has tried to stop His reaching the people of earth.

We see Jesus as a mighty warrior. Yet, He rides on a donkey and the people acclaim Him as a mighty man of God. He never fought a war where He could have proven His strength in battle, like David, His forefather, did. He disdained the implements of war, preferring the Word of God to protect Him. His enemies hounded Him and would try to destroy His credibility by using words. But Jesus, who spoke the Words of God, needed only the sword of the Word of God to protect Him. He is called a man of peace, yet He has provoked many wars worldwide!

The message that Jesus brings is one of peace, yet those Words enter into the minds of people. The Words change the way people see the rest of the world. Those who have received His Holy Spirit become His peaceful warriors, who take up the cross of Jesus to bring peace to a sinful world.

PEOPLE WHO LIVE IN A LAWLESS SOCIETY FEAR FOR THEMSELVES

There hath no temptation taken you but such as is common to man: but God is faithful, who will not suffer you to be tempted above that ye are able; but will with the temptation also make a way to escape, that ye may be able to bear it.

(I CORINTHIANS 10:13, KJV)

March 18, 1999

My soul escapes like a bird out of the snare of the fowler! Jesus is the one who makes this possible! Because of the wicked ways of the people, they can easily be snared by some temptation. They do not like following after the laws and regulations that are placed on them, so they rebel against any law that hinders them from doing that which pleases them.

It doesn't matter if the law is of value to them! There are many laws that people applaud, especially when someone else has been breaking the law, causing a problem. It is at times like these when they are staunch supporters of the law. They demand that true justice be done.

They cry to others about how others are breaking the law. They want support to help them cause others to obey the law. They may even go so far as to ask God to intervene on their behalf. It isn't that they believe in God in any special way, but they want to have their own way so badly that they will try any avenue to get their way.

If one doesn't believe in obeying laws, why do they try to hold others to a standard higher than the one they are willing to follow? It isn't that they can't follow the law, it is that abiding by the law can be too demanding. When they would prefer to do as they please, obeying the law can be a bother. It isn't even worth considering when someone wants to do something badly enough.

Then why have laws? If no one wants to abide by the laws and they are considered too restraining by the people, why make laws? Laws need to be made so that lawbreakers can be caught and made to obey the law or lose their freedom. When the penalty is powerful enough, people will think twice before they break a law. They will consider the consequences and obey the law even if they feel as if that law is a foolish law. Indeed, every law that is made has been given because people do not govern themselves.

People who live in a lawless society fear for themselves. People do tend to be rowdy and do those things that please them at the expense of others. They have not taken into consideration the detriment to other people. So, too many laws are passed that can be used as snares for the innocent by overzealous lawmakers.

JESUS COMES UNTO THOSE
WHO ASK OF HIM

And said unto them, Thus it is written, and thus it behooved
Christ to suffer, and to rise from the dead the third day: And
that repentance and remission of sins should be preached in
his name among all nations, beginning at Jerusalem.

(LUKE 24:46–47, KJV)

March 19, 1999

Hear my prayer, oh Lord, attend unto my prayer! You are the hope of all mankind. There is no other who can bring us to eternal salvation but Jesus Christ. As we look at the religions of the world, we see the bondage that people put on themselves in the name of their god! Yet, they really have very little true hope of reaching the point that their god can give to them.

Many unknown things can come about when a person is fervent in prayer. In all religions, one is asked to pray to their deity. They have great expectations that they will receive that which they ask. They find that there is strength in believing in their deity.

It is always helpful when there are several people who join together in faith. They know that what they believe must be true because others are a support to them. They love their deity because there is no other one whom they can trust to tell all of their problems and secrets. A deity listens, and often, a person sees results from praying.

Yet, there can be an emptiness that follows a longtime prayer, when there is no answer to bring them comfort.

In all religions, one must have a strength of character to guide them. The guidelines can be cumbersome and of little help to them. If a religion is burdensome, then it is more conceptualized by man than sent from God. People have always had a need to call upon someone or something to help them answer the problems of life.

All too often, these problems are manmade. People sin and, in so doing, bring a burden to their minds, bodies, and souls. There is no way that praying can bring relief until that person decides to really examine the source of their problem. Then they must repent or turn away from that which sorely depresses them. The only way they can be free is to free themselves from the burden of sin that they have placed upon themselves.

Jesus comes to those who ask of Him. He helps teach them ways that will set them free from those things that burden them. The mind is free! It can wander where it wills! The body is not; it is held by time and space. The body brings discipline to the mind. Life is reality; Jesus gives people the answers they really need.

WE PREPARE FOR AN ETERNITY IN JESUS

Behold, bless ye the LORD, all ye servants of the LORD, which by night stand in the house of the LORD. Lift up your hands in the sanctuary, and bless the LORD.

(PSALM 134:1–2, KJV)

March 20, 1999

Come bless the Lord, all ye children of the Lord! Who stand by night in the House of the Lord! Although dark times may fall on the children of God, Jesus is strong enough to defend them. They have gotten to know Jesus in a powerful way and they have enough faith and knowledge of Him to stay steadfast in Him.

Is there fear? Whenever people worry for the future, their beliefs, or their lives, there is fear! They are confused that righteousness has not won by its merit alone. They know Jesus, but what has happened to the other people in the world who have turned their backs on Him? In their hearts, they know that Jesus is the only way to peace and contentment, but the people who have become worldly do not understand the significance of the righteousness of God.

These people who see Jesus as their only truth, salvation, and hope receive faith enough to stand. They know the best that can happen to them, and they know the worst! No matter what happens, their faith in Jesus will help them cope, no matter which way

137

they are blown by the spirit of the times. Jesus remains steadfast in their hearts and minds. They find that He brings them peace in a society driven mad by sin.

Goodness and mercy shall follow me all the days of my life. I shall dwell in the house of my God and He shall bring me contentment. Life is precious to me as are those people that I love. Oh, that Jesus would spread His love over them, to let them know the peace and contentment that He brings to those who wait upon Him.

In a world where people are driven by their physical desires, it is satisfying to know that while we are in this world, we are of another world. That world is not disappointing! It is a world where we will find peace and contentment. We have struggled with our flesh and have won our battle. We stand ready to receive that which Jesus has prepared for His children.

We have no fear except fear itself, and we will not panic or run from that which is yet unseen. We will stand and fight a good battle, letting those who know us see that faith in God is a virtue; it is also knowledge because we have taken the time to know the Trinity. They are ever present inside of us. We are not blown about by any wind of doctrine. Nor does a wicked government cause us to fear. We prepare for an eternity in Jesus. None can distract us or cause us to doubt.

THE BIBLE DECLARES A GOOD NAME IS VALUABLE

Then he remembered the days of old, Moses, and his people,
saying, Where is he that brought them up out of the sea with
the shepherd of his flock? where is he that put his holy Spirit
within him? That led them by the right hand of Moses with his
glorious arm, dividing the water before them, to make him-
self an everlasting name? That led them through the deep,
as an horse in the wilderness, that they should not stumble?

(ISAIAH 63:11–13, KJV)

March 22, 1999

Jesus—there is something about that name! The names of people carry different types of power with them. Each country has
its own powerful names that make them respected by the people of the nation. When people hear the name, they know what
to expect from that person. The Bible declares a good name is
valuable. A person should respect the name that they have and
endeavor to keep it untarnished. In that way, they can ensure that
their children will not have to work diligently to make their family
name respected.

There is no finer example than the Bible for this. The first name
of certain people in the Bible reflect the characteristics of that
person. When one hears that name, they immediately know what

that person represents. They will always be known for their deeds, good or bad.

The name Moses always brings forth the image of a powerful character. Although he was born of a Hebrew family, he had all the advantages of the ruling people of Egypt. The rulers of Egypt still receive respect today. Although the line of the Pharaohs had passed away, the greatness of those people still carry on through the centuries. These people were known to be great builders. Their handiwork is still in view today, for all to see.

Moses rose to greatness through these famous leaders. Yet, it was his connection with the Hebrew people that had made him prominent in history. It wasn't his education in the greatest schools of the time that made his name remembered, it was the role he played as a great leader of a nomadic tribe that brought him his glory.

To lead a people out of Egypt and through a desert for forty years took all the training that he had. God was with him, but there were things that he needed to know that would make him strong enough to guide these people out of their slavery.

We see Jesus, not taught by the great schools of the time, able to lead the world into eternal glory. He had a different type of teacher. He did not have the type of education that Moses had in royal schools, but was endowed by the Holy Spirit of God that led Him forward to bring salvation to the people of the world.

THERE ARE LINES TO BE DRAWN AS TO HOW A PERSON MUST LIVE IN SOCIETY

And it came to pass on the morrow, that Moses said unto the people, Ye have sinned a great sin: and now I will go up unto the LORD; peradventure I shall make an atonement for your sin. And Moses returned unto the LORD, and said, Oh, this people have sinned a great sin, and have made them gods of gold. Yet now, if thou wilt forgive their sin—; and if not, blot me, I pray thee, out of thy book which thou hast written. And the LORD said unto Moses, Whosoever hath sinned against me, him will I blot out of my book.

(EXODUS 32:30–33, KJV)

March 23, 1999

Let us sing of our Redeemer, on the cross He died for me. He sealed my pardon and set me free! Free! How could a man who lived so long ago set anyone free? And what does a person need to be set free from? Not everybody gets to live a life that is holy before God. They are tempted to commit many grievances against God, other people, and themselves. Not everyone feels guilty because they have sinned. They have accepted sin as a way of life, especially when they were raised in a society where sin is of importance only when one gets caught in sin.

Ignorance of the importance of sin in one's life can spread

throughout society. The more lenient society is with sinners, the more sins will prosper. There are advantages in society to be able to sin and get away with it. It is an advantage over the person who obeys law and order. They restrain themselves when they think it is proper to do so. They maintain a righteous attitude toward God, society, and themselves.

How can one have a righteous attitude about themselves? They want to treat other people as it benefits God, society, and themselves. If they respect themselves and will not place themselves in any danger, they are watching carefully over their name and belongings.

Just as they would not want anything to happen to their things, they realize that others are careful over their possessions. One must have a respectful attitude of themselves. They may never stand out among other people as someone who is great, but who they are and what they do is important to them. They will go the extra mile for others, and they will also place themselves in a position of respect. If they do not care for themselves, they cannot expect other people to honor them.

There are limits to one's opinion of oneself. It is not right to take from someone else that which belongs to others. One must not be greedy and self-serving. There are lines to be drawn as to how a person must live in society. It is a common saying that one should use good judgment! How does one know when one's judgment is good? Scripture is the guideline that a person may follow. Although the Bible mentions many people who sinned and showed poor judgment, it also uses these people as examples of the consequences of sin.

Sin Is an Addictive Thing!

For the wages of sin is death; but the gift of God is eternal life through Jesus Christ our Lord.

(Romans 6:23, KJV)

March 24, 1999

We will sing of our Redeemer! On the cross He died for me! He was a sacrifice so that all people could be free! They do not need to be held accountable to sin! They are free to do what is right at all times.

Even after the sacrifice of the life of Jesus, people still refuse to listen to the message that Jesus brings. They enjoy sin! They don't really care if they are hampered in living a peaceful life. They find sin to be exciting. Sin may be enjoyable for a while, but there comes a time when the darkness of sin covers one like a blanket. They cannot pierce that darkness; it has control over them. They are in torment and miserable. They want to escape the problems their life of sin has brought to them.

Will Jesus hear their cries? Yes! Will He care? Yes! Will they be saved? Only if they turn away from that which torments them. Sin is an addictive thing! Although they are aware of the misery they are in, sin draws them back to it. Wasn't it fun to do those things? There were always other people who laughed with them. They were never held in contempt by their fellow merrymakers!

Although they could not be really trusted, they would share the good as long as someone else would pay the price! They would compile wicked things and then destroy those who had lost favor with them. There were no rules or laws that they were made to obey. They each care only for their own welfare and the vile needs they had acquired. All are miserable! They speak of better times, when they were young and innocent. They shed tears over their lost life and the people whom they had hurt over the years. They still believe that they are good, but they only need a sympathetic, warm, loving person who will come and save them from themselves. Yes, they hate rules and laws! Yes, they hate any authority figure who would impose laws on them!

So, they don't really desire change. They just want someone who will play with them, like they have enjoyed throughout their lives. They believe that, inside their hearts, they are never really sinful, just carefree and misunderstood. Why, any day they could change to be a righteous person, admired by all!

The truth is that only Jesus can really change the character that has become so loathsome. There are no outside forces that can change the vile thing that they have become. There has to be a cleansing from within; only a change of heart can reverse the wickedness that has grown so large that it has polluted their whole being. One cannot look at other people and expect them to make them be respectful and good. It must come from within them and their true desire to please God.

They first rebelled against authority when they were children. When they were teenagers, laws were made to be broken. Parents and authority figures were to be tricked and lied to. Yet, they paid the price with their lives. Jesus is their only hope.

WAR IS ONE OF THESE TIMES

He hath put forth his hands against such as be at peace with him: he hath broken his covenant. The words of his mouth were smoother than butter, but war was in his heart: his words were softer than oil, yet were they drawn swords. Cast thy burden upon the LORD, and he shall sustain thee: he shall never suffer the righteous to be moved.

(PSALM 55:20–22, KJV)

March 25, 1999

Those who believe in Jesus Christ will be strengthened by Him in their hour of need. There are times when life can become cruel and hard. Situations become bigger than the people. They no longer have control of their lives. They are swept away by the trouble of the times.

War is one of these times. When a person loves their country and the way that they live, they do not desire to see change. They would live their lives the way that they want to all the days of their lives, but war rears its ugly head and times change the way a person lives!

War does bring change, for it changes the way that people obey the laws. Laws are meant for peaceful nations, to keep order in the country. War brings a survival attitude among the people, and they change to fit the climate of the time. They want the war to end, and those who have begun the war to go away and leave

145

them alone. But conditions in their once-understandable land will be changed forever. There can never be the same atmosphere that these people once enjoyed. The world has become smaller in the minds of the people because people in all lands are aware of what is happening worldwide. They are no longer a certain nation that cares only for itself. They have become citizens of the world, and they are expected to know of the problems that affect all mankind worldwide.

As long as one nation is happy and well-cared for, the peace that they have can still be threatened by other nations seeking to take what they have. There are those who think that just caring for oneself is not sufficient; that as a world community, each nation deserves what the richest nation has. They do not feel that a nation should be able to have prosperity if there are those who are suffering anywhere else in the world!

We must ask about the responsibility of other nations toward their own people. One is not to covet one's neighbor's goods. If they want what their neighbors have, they should work toward that end, and not be enveloped in jealousy. Jealousy causes wars that destroy many people. Each land has many special features; those features should be explored and used to care for the people who live there.

Jesus Was the True Son of God and He Made Himself Known, Just as God Predicted He Would

> *And it shall come to pass, that every soul, which will not hear that prophet, shall be destroyed from among the people. Yea, and all the prophets from Samuel and those that follow after, as many as have spoken, have likewise foretold of these days. Ye are the children of the prophets, and of the covenant which God made with our fathers, saying unto Abraham, And in thy seed shall all the kindreds of the earth be blessed.*
>
> *(ACTS 3:23–25, KJV)*

March 26, 1999

Just sing my song, my Savior God to Thee! How great Thou art! How great Thou art. The Lord Jesus Christ has let Himself be known to the people of earth. He came, just as the Prophets of old foretold. He was the true Son of God and He made Himself known, just as God predicted He would. He has proven over and over again that His ways are beneficial for mankind, and those people who believe in Him and follow Him are a blessed people!

Persecution has always been a problem for Christians. There are many unbelievers who rise up in hate against them. They fear Christians and they want to destroy them. The unbelievers are full of hate, and they follow Christians wherever they go, purposefully trying to destroy them. Christians have a strong moral character

147

that give them strength in their time of need. Their faith in God place them above others. They see life in a different way and they have a great love for God.

It is the Holy Spirit that dwells within them, that helps them recognize the way that Jesus acts within them. They know that Jesus is true, and that He remains steadfast throughout the years. His policy is the best policy, and He imputes moral character inside of them. They may face all manner of perils, but when Jesus is within them, they have the courage to face everything that confronts them.

With sadness, they see Jesus at the cross. They cannot really imagine the pain that He suffered. One can be unrealistic when they state that they feel other's pain. They cannot. One must actually feel intense pain to know what it really feels like. Still, one may see Jesus on the cross and they know that His lone death was sufficient to redeem them from all their past sin; that through the life of Jesus, they have eternal glory in Him. He is the One who cheated death for all who follow after him. Jesus stands out as the true lover of the souls of mankind.

At this time of the year, Jesus and the cross He bore are brought to our minds. He has been around 2,000 years, and during that time, many people have been touched by His grace. He has never lost His redemptive power to save mankind. Those who hear Him are touched by Him. He still has the same saving power; it has not diminished through the centuries!

If One doesn't Emit the Presence of Jesus, Then They Need to Work upon That Sin That Holds Them Captive

Wherefore we would have come unto you, even I Paul, once and again; but Satan hindered us. For what is our hope, or joy, or crown of rejoicing? Are not even ye in the presence of our Lord Jesus Christ at his coming? For ye are our glory and joy.

(I THESSALONIANS 2:18–20, KJV)

March 27, 1999

My Jesus is here! Lift up your hands and feel His holy presence! Jesus is here. He walks among us daily. No matter where a person goes in the world, Jesus is with that person! He lives in their hearts and He makes them whole. He loves them! They are His because they have taken on His nature. If His nature is within us, then we are His. As we go about our daily lives, He walks among us!

If one doesn't emit the presence of Jesus, then they need to work on that sin that holds them captive. Jesus is made known by His moral values. There are many people who would be like Jesus. They think that the work He did for mankind is exceptional. They do not think that they can emulate His goodness. They feel it was

149

sufficient that Jesus saved their souls. The responsibility was His and not theirs; so, if they sin, the sacrifice that Jesus made was sufficient.

Yes, and no—the idea they have is only partially correct. The sacrifice of the life of Jesus is acceptable to God for all sin. But for a person to commit the same sin over and over again is insulting the sacrifice that Jesus made for us. The mind of a person is quick; they are able to learn and change things. They are made by Jesus in a certain way, so there is much to be expected of them. Since He is the Creator, He knows what abilities each person possesses. They are able to do that which He has declared they can do. He does not expect them to sin constantly and presume that Jesus will always forgive them.

All too often, it becomes easy to break a law that Jesus has declared necessary for one's salvation. When people look to Jesus for help and protection, they should look at themselves to see if there is any sin found in them. Of course people can sin and be unaware that it is sin. These sins can cause problems for a person because their sinning often includes breaking a law. If they get caught breaking a law, they will be held accountable for breaking that law. There is no way they will be excused from the penalty of the law.

Jesus is grace-laden! When people break the law and they find out about it later, they must repent for breaking that law. In repentance there is forgiveness. The penalty has been paid by Jesus.

It Is Easy to Make Promises!

*And Joshua called for them, and he spake unto them, saying,
Wherefore have ye beguiled us, saying, We are very far from
you; when ye dwell among us? Now therefore ye are cursed,
and there shall none of you be freed from being bondmen,
and hewers of wood and drawers of water for the house of
my God. And they answered Joshua, and said, Because it was
certainly told thy servants, how that the LORD thy God commanded his servant Moses to give you all the land, and to
destroy all the inhabitants of the land from before you, therefore we were sore afraid of our lives because of you, and have
done this thing.*

(JOSHUA 9:22–24, KJV)

March 29, 1999

We shall gather together in His name! We shall rejoice in Jesus our Savior. He is our only hope and in Him may we trust. He gave His Word long ago that He would prepare a place for those people who follow after Him. His covenant with those who believe upon Him is still true! It is still in effect. He is able to perform the things that He has promised!

It is easy to believe in promises that people make to others. It is easy to make promises! It isn't easy to fulfill them. Some of the simplest problems that people have appear to be those that certain people know how to fix. But there comes a time when these problems become complex, and they are not as simple as they may seem.

Too often, the person with the problem misrepresents it. They do not tell the whole truth on the subject. If people, who value their word, know the solution to the basic problem and offer to help, but have been deceived, are they still held accountable for their word? It all depends on the morals of the person. People's words are of importance to them. They will try to fulfill their word.

Joshua is an example of this in the Old Testament. When a few people—who knew their nation was in danger because of the advancing Israelites—lied, tricking the Israelites into making a pact with them to save themselves from danger, the Israelites remained true to their word. How did the Israelites hold these people responsible for their trickery? They made them slaves, or else they would have annihilated them. Instead of death these people sold themselves and their future generations into slavery.

Today we see the same thing happening to people in the world. Because they know that they are set for slaughter, they make deals that take away their freedom. They know that, for a period of time, they will not have an opportunity to be a free people, but they have been given their lives! They have stooped low in order to eventually gain freedom from a fierce enemy.

Anyone who holds another people captive will pay a price for this in the long run. These captives will never be integrated into the general society, but there will come a time when they can barter for the freedom of their people.

It Is a Test of a Person's Beliefs When They Can Reject the Accepted Ideas of the Time and Refuse to Abide By Them

Behold, bless ye the LORD, all ye servants of the LORD, which by night stand in the house of the LORD. Lift up your hands in the sanctuary, and bless the LORD. The LORD that made Heaven and earth bless thee out of Zion.

(PSALM 134:1–3, KJV)

March 30, 1999

Come bless the Lord, all ye servants of the Lord, who stand by night in the house of the Lord. People who believe in Jesus may tremble when they see an enemy stand before them. They may gather together and wait for the dawn to break. The hours creep by when it is dark and no one is sure what will happen to them even when dawn comes!

This is the time for Christians who have determined to be called children of God to stand firm. Life means nothing to them. Jesus and His ways are paramount to them. All has been given to Jesus and they are in His care.

This is a time when people trust in Jesus for their lives. There have been times when they are spared and they live a long life, content in their choice!

153

Then there are times when their lives are snuffed out because of the wickedness and fear that hateful people hold against them. People are comfortable with those who act and think as they do. But when strangers have other ideas that threaten them, people will strike out at those people who act differently than they do.

It is a test of a person's beliefs when they can reject the accepted ideas of the time and refuse to abide by them. They declare that they are right and others are wrong. When this happens, they bring problems on themselves. They become a threat to others who secretly have an inward fear that they could be wrong. They fight to prove that they are right, that even if the system they believe in is flawed, they will adhere to the status quo.

Jesus brings light and understanding to the people. He lets them know the truth when they see it. He brings them confidence that justice will prevail. If justice does not prevail in this world, it will do so in people's afterlives, so remaining faithful to Jesus gives them a strong determination that they are survivors and will triumph in the end.

The time of darkness will pass as Jesus spreads His light to all who will have an ear to hear and eyes to see. He brings hope that the most average of people will be able to come unto His marvelous understanding of the truth. Jesus dispels all darkness and gives His people hope and encouragement.

The Relationship Suffers because There Have Been Too Many Rejections and Resentments Over the Years

O LORD, by these things men live, and in all these things is the life of my spirit: so wilt thou recover me, and make me to live. Behold, for peace I had great bitterness: but thou hast in love to my soul delivered it from the pit of corruption: for thou hast cast all my sins behind thy back. For the grave cannot praise thee, death cannot celebrate thee: they that go down into the pit cannot hope for thy truth.

(ISAIAH 38:16–18, KJV)

March 31, 1999

He is Lord! He has risen from the dead and He is Lord. We look unto Jesus for the needs in our lives. There are many times when we find ourselves upset by those people who are around us. They are the ones we are supposed to love, and that love becomes strained by everyday differences. Neither may be wrong but they cannot agree on a solution. They can become estranged because each has an answer but the answers are different!

One of the parties is bound to be hurt. There is a good chance each will become upset with the other. This is no time for one who gets his way to be superior. That answer may not have been the best solution, but the one was the stronger of the two and did that which that one wanted to do!

No matter what, there will always be a feeling of restraint between the two because they were not happy with the outcome. Both retained their own solutions, whether or not the solution was resolved in their favor. There will be resentment, and the one who lost will hold resentment deep within them. Although they may never mention it again, they will feel angry on the inside. They will never respond to the matter that caused that inward hurt!

Jesus would have people forgive each other in love. They are to take their loss as if they never had an opinion in the first place. They are to assess the situation and see the futility of changing the whole matter. But if this type of thing happens too often, love is replaced by anger and hate. The relationship suffers because there have been too many rejections and resentments built over the years. The person who has always deferred to the stronger person builds up a list of hurts that cannot be easily resolved.

Yet each person feels that they have allowed other people to have their ways on many occasions. They each have their list of hurts. They do not forget! In moments of anger, their minds can flare up and relive the times of anger and resentment. Although they may never speak a word, they retain these times of conflict in their minds.

People should be responsible in their actions toward others. They should realize how it feels to be rejected on any subject. If they don't think their opinion is really appreciated, they should turn their cheek and not respond, averting any conflict.

THE TIME OF BEING MORAL HAS DISAPPEARED

From whence come wars and fightings among you? come they not hence, even of your lusts that war in your members? Ye lust, and have not: ye kill, and desire to have, and cannot obtain: ye fight and war, yet ye have not, because ye ask not. Ye ask, and receive not, because ye ask amiss, that ye may consume it upon your lusts.

(JAMES 4:1–3, KJV)

April 1, 1999

Dear Jesus, we need You now! Those characteristics that you died for, for the people of earth, seem to be of little value to them now! They seek to fulfill their own desires and lusts. They see no need for keeping anything away from themselves. If they want it, they buy it or do it. They place few or no restrictions upon themselves. Because of this, they have little in reserve that keeps them able to survive in times of trouble.

When the people or their leaders wanted something, they would take it and lie about it. If they are caught while doing it, they blame everyone else but themselves. They blame their government, friends, or family. They see no reason why they should suffer for their sins or wickedness. They were just caught doing something that was breaking someone else's law, and they decry the fact that they are being held responsible for it.

157

The laws of God that have held the world in restraint from wickedness are considered to be for another era. The time of being moral has disappeared. The person had best beware of others because their words are valueless to others. Truth and justice are in the eyes of the beholder. If they fight for their country, they had better look at the character of the people who are running their country. Then they will know how safe they really are! If their leaders feel that the soldiers are expendable, then there shouldn't be any person who is willing to take a chance by serving their country.

What a sad day for a nation when there is no one willing to place themselves in harm's way to defend that which is good for the country. If the leaders themselves sell out their own people to foreigners, why should anyone place themselves in jeopardy for these wicked leaders? So the country flounders because the ways of God are mocked.

The laws of God have kept people in peace and trust throughout history. Yes, there have been confrontations between disagreeing parties, but there has always been a code of law that has kept mayhem from taking over. Now, there are no restraints in what one group can do to another. The codes that held people to some type of civil rules are being destroyed. No one is safe! If they have something of value, it is in danger of being taken from them. Anarchy rules the land!

They See Evil for
What It Truly Is

And ye shall know the truth, and the truth shall make you free. They answered him, We be Abraham's seed, and were never in bondage to any man: how sayest thou, Ye shall be made free? Jesus answered them, Verily, verily, I say unto you, Whosoever committeth sin is the servant of sin.

(*JOHN 8:32–34, KJV*)

April 2, 1999

Jesus is the rock of my salvation; His banner over us is love. It is difficult to find someone who always knows the truth of a matter. When they say something to you, you know that what they say is true. There is no guile found in them. They know that the truth can be painful, but when the truth has been known, a problem can be dealt with and changed.

Jesus is all truth! He talks to us through His Holy Spirit. In the gentlest fashion, He leads people to truth, but people resist truth! They enjoy what they are doing. They may even know that it is bad for them, but they have hope that, in the end, they can change that which was wrong to right.

Through persistence a person may get what they had wanted so strongly. They may marry that person who has a shady character. They may get what they wanted through trickery, but that which is bad at the start will not automatically be made good. If a person, through evil intentions, gets the person who is hoping to change them for the better, they will find themselves living with someone they do not really like. They will not change their true character. They have not been trained to live a God-fearing life. They are who they are, and change will never be fast enough to bring congeniality between these two people.

When people ask Jesus into their hearts, a subtle change takes place. If they have been truly sorry for their wicked actions and want to change, a change toward the truth will take place. As they study the Word of God, they will find out what is true. Because they want to please God, they will take the necessary steps to change themselves. The love of Jesus is constantly there, encouraging them. They can see the truth clearly! That which was once acceptable to them is repugnant. They see evil for what it truly is. They see right as a hopeful matter that can free them from sin.

People who are in trouble know that sin can ruin their lives. They know no way to escape the snare they are currently caught in, but Jesus can change their lives and set them free to like themselves and find true love.

WHEN THEY KNOCK AT THE DOOR WHERE JESUS IS, THEY SEE ALL THAT IS REQUIRED OF THEM

Give not that which is holy unto the dogs, neither cast ye your pearls before swine, lest they trample them under their feet, and turn again and rend you. Ask, and it shall be given you; seek, and ye shall find; knock, and it shall be opened unto you: For every one that asketh receiveth; and he that seeketh findeth; and to him that knocketh it shall be opened. Or what man is there of you, whom if his son ask bread, will he give him a stone?

(MATTHEW 7:6–9, KJV)

April 5, 1999

Thou art worthy to open the Book of Life. Each person is born in ignorance. They are required in their lifetime to come unto Jesus their Savior. It was through Jesus that life came to humankind. It is in Jesus that they find life eternal. He is the only One who can open up eternal life unto humankind. He has already done that long ago. Now it is up to each individual to find Jesus during one's brief stay on earth. Jesus is the door; each person is required to knock and pass through the door themselves.

Yet, it is Jesus who must answer their knocking. He has already set the door in place, now each must find that door. There are many doors that have been presented to the people of earth. Each

161

door seems attractive. People aren't too difficult to understand. They have many of the same weaknesses and strengths. People who would take advantage of them know what they want. So they concoct a scheme that can draw many unwary people to them. These people are foolish because they accept what appears to be good. If they would take time to study the problem before they accepted it, they would save themselves from danger. But they want to receive the false gold that is waiting just inside these fake doors. They willingly give of their souls to anyone who seems to have an answer for them.

When they knock at the door where Jesus is, they see all that is required of them. They must give of themselves. They must be honest and true. They must be able to stand and defend their faith against any falsehood that comes to them. They must be able to discern the good from the bad. They must know who Jesus really is before they rush to another door to see who is lurking there!

To know Jesus is to move forth in glory. Once people get to know who Jesus really is, they want to become as He is. They are willing to change from foolish beings into children of God. It is Jesus who leads them to where their souls really desire to go. He is their hope when life on Earth becomes too overwhelming for them.

In Jesus lies the strength of eternal salvation. From the moment someone is called, they feel a drawing that excites them and causes them to rush forward to receive all that Jesus has to offer.

THE ANSWERS ARE THERE!

And the devil said unto him, If thou be the Son of God, command this stone that it be made bread. And Jesus answered him, saying, It is written, That man shall not live by bread alone, but by every Word of God.

(LUKE 4:3–4, KJV)

April 6, 1999

Where are we going, Lord? What are we doing, Lord? Who is the Light? This part of a poem was given to us when we became born again long ago. Indeed, these questions were in our hearts. The awesomeness of the Holy Spirit encompassed us with His love. He has been giving us the answers ever since!

Many different things have taken place over the years, yet the love of Jesus still remains strong within us! We seek to please Jesus more every day. We see Him in everything that is good in human nature. We have grown to know Him and He has remained faithful through the years. That which He has instilled within us remains steadfast. He is truth! We worship and adore Him because He is truly God. In Him, there is no variance of the truth He has given to us. We only expand upon that which He has taught us.

The knowledge that comes from Jesus through the Holy Spirit expands daily. He lets us see that the nature of people does not change throughout the years. They commit the same sins generation after generation. Each person in his own time will face the

163

same problems that their forefathers have faced. The way that they judge them and handle them will reflect on the spirit of the times. Many of these problems appear in Scripture. The answers in Scripture tell how each generation should face the problems that face them. They tell about the way that some people handled them. They tell of the problems that people had to face when they broke from the ways of God and did that which seemed right in the eyes of the people.

The same temptations are there. The same way that people choose to answer them are there. The outcome of the people and the various nations' choices are there. The answers are there! No one can claim ignorance from the sins and problems that people face century after century.

Just because the scenario has changed doesn't mean the story line is different. People fall for the same wicked tricks that people have taken part in over the ages. People would declare that they didn't know. If they are in ignorance, then they aren't in touch with the Trinity. They should make it their business to know.

JESUS IS THE PROOF
THAT GOD IS REAL!

How beautiful upon the mountains are the feet of him that bringeth good tidings, that publisheth peace; that bringeth good tidings of good, that publisheth salvation; that saith unto Zion, Thy God reigneth!

(ISAIAH 52:7, KJV)

April 7, 1999

How lovely on the mountains are the feet of Him who brings good news. Everybody likes people who bring good news. In a world where there seems to be many disasters, a person who bears good news is fun to be around. They are not prating fools who strive to make people laugh for the sake of laughter. These people are upbeat, finding the best in everyday life.

Jesus brought good news! He came as a prophet, bringing the news that God had kept His promise to give a Messiah to the world. Because of the life of Jesus, all people can rejoice in Him. God is real! How many people have searched their whole lifetimes looking for the truth of a matter? When they find truth, they rejoice in it! Jesus is the proof that God is real! There is someone greater than man who loves and cares for the people of earth.

The whole world is being filled with people. Although there are billions of people, a person can walk through life never touching another person's soul. They want desperately to be special in someone else's eyes. Yet, they fail to make the contact needed to reach anyone.

It is a time like this when Jesus becomes so valuable to someone. He reaches into their souls and lets them know that He loves them. They were not an accident of life; they are someone who matters, and they are precious to Him.

But one cannot touch Jesus! They yearn for another human being who can touch their physical being and let them know that the love of Jesus is found in mankind. Each person needs to be nourished and cared for! Why can't love be found in abundance among the children of Jesus?

Love is a learned behavior! A person is taught how to care for others. Liking people takes a lot of work. Everybody is proud of the ideas and ways that they have learned in order to cope with life. They are made up of many different influences. They accept some ideas and reject others. This is not love! This is learning the ways of man on the earth.

There were many crafts the people knew about when Jesus walked on the earth. He learned how to be a carpenter at His father's knee. He did not learn about the ways of God through him. His knowledge of love came from God. He touched the people because of His willingness to share that which God taught Him. Yet, through Joseph, He learned how people must care for themselves. He was not two different personalities. He was a combination of both. People must learn how to cope with life through the physical part of their nature. They learn about God through their Spiritual nature. Love is a composition of both parts of a person.

WILL THESE PEOPLE USE THE SPIRIT OF THE TIMES AS THEIR EXCUSE?

> *For if thou wert cut out of the olive tree which is wild by nature, and wert grafted contrary to nature into a good olive tree: how much more shall these, which be the natural branches, be grafted into their own olive tree? For I would not, brethren, that ye should be ignorant of this mystery, lest ye should be wise in your own conceits; that blindness in part is happened to Israel, until the fulness of the Gentiles be come in. And so all Israel shall be saved: as it is written, There shall come out of Sion the Deliverer, and shall turn away ungodliness from Jacob:*
>
> *(ROMANS 11:24–26, KJV)*

April 8, 1999

Jesus is the rock of my salvation. His banner over us is love. He has not seen the sins that have been committed against Him. He only sees a deluded, lost people who have not tried to really know Him. He is willing at all times to welcome them into His Kingdom. But the people see Him as being weak and they think they are able to manipulate His goodness.

People have their own ideas about who Jesus is. Although they do not really want to share in His ways, they do want His mercy and grace. They want Jesus, if He is true, to overlook everything that they have done against Him and their fellow man. They want

167

acceptance from everyone. They do not like to pay the penalty for their sins.

Jesus will not disagree with the Father! If God has demanded certain things throughout history from people, He is not able to change the laws that He has governed them by. The people of today are not to be treated with favor. They are the same as people who lived in the past. Today, people consider themselves to be smarter than those who lived before them. The requirements will be as stringent today as they were in times past. Today's people will be held accountable even if they feel that they should be excused from all sin.

Because of their arrogance, they will have a more difficult time knowing who Jesus truly is. They will be kept in their blindness because they do not have the will to seek the truth. The people have been drawn away by their own lusts and they refuse to change. If God wants them He must make provisions for them, they opine.

Will these people use the spirit of the times as their excuse? They may, but they will not get away with it! In every age, there have been seducing spirits that have been given the job of drawing people away from God and His righteousness. People have had the ability to turn to God and repent from sin in every age.

Jesus can come to the most sin weary of people. He can help them understand good from evil. He can make them hate sin. They can live righteously in His eyes. They have no acceptable excuse to lose their soul because of their stubbornness. Jesus stands like a beacon to the weary travelers on earth. He draws them unto Him and they find rest in Him. He never fails to give them respite from those sins that beset their souls.

JESUS REINSTATED THE
TEN COMMANDMENTS

And he said unto them, These are the words which I spake
unto you, while I was yet with you, that all things must be
fulfilled, which were written in the law of Moses, and in the
prophets, and in the psalms, concerning me.

(LUKE 24:44, KVJ)

April 9, 1999

Jesus, You are the lover of my soul! Not mine only, but every person who was ever born and comes unto You receives Your love.
One would declare that there is never enough love to go around.
There are times when it seems like some people find precedence
over others; that Jesus favors them with many fine gifts and special love.

It is true that people receive special gifts from Jesus. To those
people, much is given but much is expected in return. One may
look at all the select people in the Bible. God spoke to them, but
they were the ones who had to find a way to do that which was
asked of them. There were few minor tasks set before them. Many
of the tasks were life-changing for the people who were to follow
after these special people of God.

Who hasn't sympathized with Moses, Joshua, Isaiah, and others? Each was sent to do a task that the average person would
never have an idea how to accomplish. It is one thing to receive

169

the message. It is another to go about bringing about the change. Who could lead an army of people through a scorching desert? Not only did Moses need to find the way, he needed to contend with the people and their thoughts.

Jesus also came to lead a large people out of apostasy and change the way that they viewed God. Over the centuries, the people became mired in legalism. They continuously enmeshed themselves in legalism that would bring problems to them. They did not seek God in the way that God had asked of them. They tried to improve the ways of God by adding different standards for themselves. They caused themselves to stand out among the nations!

In the time of Jesus, the Romans came and conquered the land. The Romans brought law. It was man-made legalism that brought equality to the masses. People had rights, and they could appeal their cause to higher courts that could alter the charges brought against them. These laws would spread across the known nations and make people equal in the eyes of men.

Jesus reinstated the Ten Commandments. The people could follow the Roman law. The Commandments helped bring obedience to the law to the world. One could obey God and the law of the land at the same time. One set of laws did not hinder the other. Together it made for better government.

It is difficult to rule over rebellious people. Abiding by the law is essential for any society. When people know and respect the law, they live in a safer society. Everyone thrives in safety.

Honoring One's Parents Must Come from Careful Teaching of a Child

Honour thy father and thy mother: that thy days may be long upon the land which the Lord thy God giveth thee.

(EXODUS 20:12, KJV)

April 10, 1999

We give Thee thanks, dear Jesus, for the wisdom, knowledge, and understanding that You give to us, Your children. We love You, much like all children do who depend upon You daily. It is difficult for a parent at times to love a child when the child is not open to understanding, when the child would rather argue than listen to the advice that the parent gives!

There comes a time when the parent just walks away and lets the child work through the problems. When the child has failed at the task that was given, the child will become more open to suggestions that a parent may have. Then the child can grow to be all that the parent had hoped.

Too often, changes come late in life. Once the child has suffered enough, there will be a willingness to accept the changes that need to be made. Has the advice that the parent given to the child been beneficial? Although it may take a while, the child will eventually see all that the parent was trying to communicate. The child will see that the love of a parent is a beautiful thing, that if there is competition with a parent, it is usually a child vying for autonomy.

It has been recently said that no one wants to work anymore. People want everything they own to be the best, but they do not have regard for it once they have received it. They take it as just something to own. It loses its value to them once they have purchased it and used it!

One should ask themselves about the value of things. Things steal away one's life. People press forward to acquire things for themselves, things they don't need that are just attractive, wrapped up in a package that is exciting to open. We look at people who greedily reach for all manner of things, hoping to find an answer for their emptiness.

Parents can teach children the value of things, whether they are great or small. Honoring one's parents must come from careful teaching of a child. If a parent has little regard for their own word, then how can they expect anyone else to respect them? A child must learn to trust the words of a parent before the child is grown. If the parents tell a child stories that prove to be untrue, then the child will never be able to trust them as adults. Love comes from the respect that one person has for the other, adult or child.

They Have Seen Jesus' Sacrifice; the Most Wonderful Thing That Humans Have Is Their Lives

But made himself of no reputation, and took upon him the form of a servant, and was made in the likeness of men: And being found in fashion as a man, he humbled himself, and became obedient unto death, even the death of the cross. Wherefore God also hath highly exalted him, and given him a name which is above every name:

(PHILIPPIANS 2:7–9, KJV)

April 12, 1999

Jesus is the rock of my salvation! His banner over us is love! We have learned how to trust Him over the years. Failure may be found in us, but He gives us the courage to stand and remain firm in Him. As long as there is life there is hope. Jesus gives us hope, not only for today but also for all the days to come.

As long as there are other people who live on this earth, we must learn to live with them. We may not like them, but they do have a right to live. People establish the code of life that they will live with. It suits them! They believe in what they are doing! Other people know certain things; they make them into guidelines for themselves. They then turn it into a code for life for themselves!

People do not need to believe in another's code of life. The code may not work for them, so they alter the code to suit themselves.

They then are working under the same code as the person before them, but they have adjusted it to be workable for them.

This is one reason why the human mind is so marvelous. It is able to adjust. One may not like doing something at first, but after understanding it comes reaping from it.

Jesus comes to those who seek Him. He comes with a certain code of ethics. People must learn how to make that code work for them. They know of the goodness of Jesus. They know that He died a horrid death on a cross so that they could enter His way of living. They often think what a terrible sacrifice it had to be to die for unethical people, but Jesus knew that He was the only one who could help them change their evil way of living.

People look at the cross and find many things that cause them to think about their lives. They would not like to die on a cross. They have seen Jesus' sacrifice; the most wonderful thing that humans have is their lives. If a person who was sinless as Jesus can be murdered because of His thoughts, and He is the only true Son of God, then how can we stand in this imperfect world?

PEOPLE, BY THE WAY THEY WERE CREATED, COULD OBEY GOD

For it pleased the Father that in him should all fulness dwell;
And, having made peace through the blood of his cross, by
him to reconcile all things unto himself; by him, I say, whether
they be things in earth, or things in heaven. And you, that
were sometime alienated and enemies in your mind by wicked
works, yet now hath he reconciled

(COLOSSIANS 1:19–21, KJV)

April 13, 1999

Please let us know Your ways, dear Jesus! Help us to be all that You would have Your people be. We long to be like You! You were holy and true! God entrusted in You the lives of His people. You satisfied God completely! God declared how content He was with the way You lived Your life on earth. There was no fault found in You!

But the people of earth complain constantly about You and the things that they think You stand for. They are unhappy about the things that You demand of them. Although You created mankind, they do not do that which is expected of them. They are openly rebellious about any restrictions that are placed upon them. Even if God has declared that which is expected of them, they resist that which is best for them! They have been rebellious since Adam and Eve!

175

People, by the way they were created, could obey God. Yet, they choose not to! They will declare their righteousness, but if they examined themselves through the eyes of God, they would be appalled by their own unrighteousness. They would see clearly how they offend God and His ways!

People have selective hearing and sight! They see and hear what they want to see and hear. They are more concerned about the way they feel about something than if they are following the ways of God. They want things to suit their way of thinking. It is great when God goes along with their thoughts! Who wouldn't want God on their side? But they fool themselves if they think that God can accept any other doctrine than the One He has given to them. In His ways, all perfection is made complete!

There have been many artistic depictions by people of Jesus on the cross. He was there, alone! His hands were pierced by nails. His feet crossed at the foot so that just one single spike held Him to the bottom of the cross! There was blood sprinkling down from His various wounds. He didn't look like a conqueror, but like a vanquished compatriot!

Are His ways right? If they were, wouldn't all people be horrified by what they see? A righteous person stripped of life. His head was bowed as if He had something to be ashamed of! If this could happen to a righteous person, how then should one feel when they see their Master slain at the hands of His enemies?

Yet, death on earth is not the curse that people think it is. It is only the gateway to where Jesus has gone. He calls His righteous people unto Him. They have seen the enemy and they have overcome!

Holy Spirit, You Are
Welcome in This Place

*Beloved, believe not every spirit, but try the spirits whether
they are of God: because many false prophets are gone out
into the world. Hereby know ye the Spirit of God: Every spirit
that confesseth that Jesus Christ is come in the flesh is of God:
And every spirit that confesseth not that Jesus Christ is come
in the flesh is not of God: and this is that spirit of antichrist,
whereof ye have heard that it should come; and even now
already is it in the world.*

(I John 4:1–3, KJV)

April 14, 1999

Holy Spirit, You are welcome in this place. People the world
over believe in spirits. They most often see them as evil spirits. They give them credit for all the evil things that happen to
them. All too often, it isn't an evil spirit that is giving them problems; it is their own incompetence. There isn't some wicked spirit
that just surprises them and attacks them just because they have
the power to do so!

There is order in the spirit world. They cannot harass some
person because they want to torment people. They are allowed to
harass a person when that person opens themselves to some type
of evil practice. This is when a person can get tormented by some
force that appears to attack them from nowhere. It seems that

177

many problems have attacked at once. When this happens, that person has not let Jesus control the individual's life. The person has welcomed evil forces in and has not disdained sin.

There are times when accidental things happen to people. This doesn't mean that they are engaged in constant evil behavior, which has begun to control them. It means that they are subject to the happenings on earth and they can be a victim of what is taking place around them.

There are times when the whole of a nation will turn to evilness. They do not seek righteousness. There will be varying degrees of evil in the land. As long as there are good people who are in the majority, the land will do well. But when most of the people seek and delight in evil, the whole of the nation will suffer.

We already are aware that when an evil society rises up in a land, injustice follows; that the people don't know right from wrong. They see sin being accepted by the majority of the people! They can be good themselves, but they are subject to the evil that befalls them. A wicked people have few values that bring about a good society. All suffer when evil is accepted and good is rejected.

When many people begin to accept wickedness, the foundation of that society cracks. It becomes so wicked that no person is safe from the wicked actions of others. They would like to think that they are above reproach, that their evilness isn't as great as some other person's but they are only deceiving themselves! A little sin brings small problems that lead to more sins, which bring bigger problems. Jesus needs to be the Lord of all the world. Worship Him in righteousness and truth!

GREAT PEOPLE OF THE BIBLE
WERE TRIED AND TESTED BECAUSE
OF THEIR CONNECTION WITH GOD

The Spirit of the Lord GOD is upon me; because the LORD hath anointed me to preach good tidings unto the meek; he hath sent me to bind up the brokenhearted, to proclaim liberty to the captives, and the opening of the prison to them that are bound; To proclaim the acceptable year of the LORD, and the day of vengeance of our God; to comfort all that mourn; To appoint unto them that mourn in Zion, to give unto them beauty for ashes, the oil of joy for mourning, the garment of praise for the spirit of heaviness; that they might be called trees of righteousness, the planting of the LORD, that he might be glorified.

(ISAIAH 61:1–3, KJV)

April 15, 1999

He is Lord! He has risen from the dead and He is Lord! It is a delight to know Jesus. He is the strength of all who know Him. When life becomes hectic, people who know Jesus can call upon Him; He gives them renewed strength. The more a person learns to trust in Jesus, the better life they lead.

People cannot do the things that Jesus did! He was the only true Son of God. There will be no other who can come in the manner that Jesus did! They will not have the Spiritual wisdom that Jesus possessed. He and the Father God were one, and that which God knew He passed on to Jesus. Jesus learned about God through His affiliation with Him. He was guided by God even before His birth. He was made safe by the help of God and the Heavenly creatures who are the servants of God.

There are many remarkable people who rise up and become great. Some people have talents and wisdom as mere children. They are of the world, but they are uneasy in the world. They do not feel like an ordinary person does. They find life easier for them and find that other people look at them as if there is something wrong with them!

Still they are forced to live their lives among people who have authority over them. They must live their lives in a modest way because they do not want to appear to be superior to the others. It can only draw more attention to them and make them feel more out of step with the rest of mankind.

It is said that people do not live up to their abilities, that they use only a small part of their brain. Still people learn to conquer that which is around them and to be content with their lot in life. People would like to have their lives directed for them, where all they would have to do was follow the direction of a mastermind.

Although God directed Jesus and talked with Him, following the ways of God wasn't easy. A person may receive directions to do something; it is not easy when working in a hostile environment. Jesus knew the ways of God, but very few of the people who surrounded Him were able to carry out the directives of God. There are always forces that want to destroy anyone who wants to change things. Great people of the Bible were tried and tested because of their connection with God.

But One's Own Personal Problems Are Birthed from Within

> *Many there be which say of my soul, There is no help for him in God. Selah. But thou, O LORD, art a shield for me; my glory, and the lifter up of mine head. I cried unto the LORD with my voice, and he heard me out of his holy hill. Selah.*
>
> *(PSALM 3:2–4, KJV)*

April 16, 1999

Jesus is my glory and the lifter of my head. "The lifter up of my head," Scripture declares. Whenever we see people who have problems, they walk with their heads bowed, as if they have a heavy weight upon them! No smile escapes their lips! They seem dark in spirit. Their problem is too heavy for them to carry. The rest of the world is abstract to them, because that which is carried in their minds overwhelms them.

When people come to Jesus, they usually have heavy problems that they can't solve. They do not know where to flee so they can escape the heavy burden that is on them. They come to Jesus for relief from that which oppresses them, day and night.

Many times the problems are widespread. People in a certain area will find that they have a local problem. They look to their government to solve their problem. They hope that they will actually profit from their situation and that the government will give them the support they need. Their situation can soon be resolved, and they feel free to discuss it with others.

But one's own personal problems are birthed from within. It is the individual's own actions that cause the problems. It is difficult to find anyone who really cares. If people have been foolish and have gotten themselves into a predicament, they will be responsible for resolving the matter!

When they become contrite enough and call upon Jesus, they can find relief from their problems. Does Jesus send finances to help them? He works on them in a different way. He, first of all, makes them realize that they have gotten themselves into their situation. They are to change and reverse the way they have been acting. They are to use the mind that God has given them to find the solution to their problem. Change is a necessity! They must have a true change of heart and begin to grow in character.

Being honest with one's creditor will help one change the way the debtor is being looked at by the creditor. They would often consider reducing the payment just so they could receive part of their money. When one is dealing with personal matters, there are spiritual matters that must be considered. These are similar to physical ones. One should make payment for the wrong they have done; Jesus is the lifter of one's head!

Each Person Has Their Own Times When They Have done Something That Is Evil

Even the righteousness of God which is by faith of Jesus Christ unto all and upon all them that believe: for there is no difference: For all have sinned, and come short of the glory of God; Being justified freely by his grace through the redemption that is in Christ Jesus:

(ROMANS 3:22–24, KJV)

April 17, 1999

Lift Jesus higher! Lift Him up for the world to see! The people become disenchanted with the ways of the world. They want to see righteousness. When someone relates a story about the way they overcame an injustice, they are happy that justice has been done!

Each person has their own times when they have done something that is evil. They are glad when they got away with it without paying a penalty for it. But their conscience can bother them all their lives, and they wish there was some way that they could resolve the matter. They would return to honesty and become clean of sin once again.

Jesus is the only One who knows the human mind. He knows that inside a person lurks the fear of one's evilness being revealed.

183

They run in fear when they think that someone may reveal that which they have done. Once a person takes part in some type of evil, they are drawn down a path of unrighteousness. They may hate it in their heart, but their mind always keeps evil as a way of escaping from their actions that cannot stand inspection.

All too often they profit from evil in some way. They see others making profits that they know are not legal. They often see the laws that govern them as too strident. They see people who do not earn their money by hard work prosper at the expense of others, so they try to figure a way around those laws so that they, too, can profit.

It is one matter when one tries to escape the laws that are made by man, it is another when they try to escape the laws of God. God knows the heart of man, and the laws that He gave to them are always profitable to those who obey them. They live a more contented, carefree life when they know and obey the laws of God. It is when they place the laws of God and the laws of the government in the same category that they become confused. Life doesn't seem to be good or free to them.

Man has ways of demanding that its people become law abiders. They can punish people and destroy them, but breaking the law of God becomes a private torture that only God and that person know. People suffer when they commit rebellion against God!

He Wanted Them to Preach the Story of God So That All People Could Join in His Eternal Splendor

That thou keep this commandment without spot, unrebuk-
able, until the appearing of our Lord Jesus Christ: Which in his
times he shall shew, who is the blessed and only Potentate,
the King of kings, and Lord of lords; Who only hath immortal-
ity, dwelling in the light which no man can approach unto;
whom no man hath seen, nor can see: to whom be honour
and power everlasting. Amen.

(I TIMOTHY 6: 14–16, KJV)

April 19, 1999

He is Lord! He has risen from the dead and He is Lord! Jesus is the ultimate ruler of all time. He did not place Himself in a lofty palace like other rulers do. He did not demand money from the people to keep Himself in beautiful clothing and to have the finest that money could buy. In fact, He did not want people to labor for Him. He wanted them to preach the story of God so that all people could join in His eternal splendor.

A King who shared His wealth among the people is what Jesus is for all who will be called by His name. One would say that any king who divided his wealth among many would soon be poor. But in the case of Jesus, those people who are called by His name enrich the Kingdom of God. The more people who believe, the

185

more generous they become, the more riches there are to distribute among the people.

Jesus is never seen as a person who is surrounded by luxury. Yet, His clothing is white and shiny. He has a golden glow about His face. He looks strong and able to help all who come to Him. There isn't anything that one may ask of Him that He is not able to provide. He has all knowledge, and He is willing to share His wisdom with anyone who inquires of Him. He doesn't demand of them, yet people who come unto Him expect to give their best unto Him.

His love reaches beyond all barriers. There isn't a person who has ever lived, who truly sought from Jesus, who was turned away! There are blessings every day that are sent out to those who seek them. When they receive them, the blessings do not shrivel away; they are subject to grow and multiply until the glory of Jesus has covered the whole of one's life.

One must understand the true reality that comes from Jesus Christ. It isn't as though there is a big cash society that God maintains and that He gives to the people who come looking for a handout. It is a mutual relationship where people would not take advantage of God. They know that giving of oneself to others spreads the goodness of God wherever His people are found. It is a wonderful world filled with the goodness of God through Jesus Christ!

HE STILL REACHES INTO THE HEARTS OF THE PEOPLE, CALLING THEM TO RIGHTEOUSNESS

Which none of the princes of this world knew: for had they known it, they would not have crucified the Lord of glory. But as it is written, Eye hath not seen, nor ear heard, neither have entered into the heart of man, the things which God hath prepared for them that love him. But God hath revealed them unto us by his Spirit: for the Spirit searcheth all things, yea, the deep things of God.

(I CORINTHIANS 2:8–10, KJV)

April 20, 1999

He is the King of kings! He is the Lord of lords! In Jesus may we place our trust. There are people who would declare that they know who Jesus truly is! They have known Him since they were children. Yet they have never really known His ways and what He really stands for. They have heard people describe Him at length, yet they do not focus on what they are saying. They see Jesus through the eyes of men, not through the eyes of God.

There is a big difference between hearing about Jesus and His great adventures on earth and looking behind the adventures to see what Jesus actually accomplished while He lived on earth. His life is described as a merciful one and as a man of sorrows, because He came to earth to die so that all people may live!

"It was His destiny!" some scholars declare. Was there another way for God to redeem His creation on earth besides death? All people know that they will die! By the time they are old, they have lived their lives in the manner that they have chosen. Life has become boring and tedious. They know that what they were to accomplish has been done. Why should they struggle with life when they are making no new gains? Nor are they interested in fighting the world to prove anything!

People like the status quo. They like things to continue as they have always been. But young people come along with different ideas. They catch the imagination of those who are their age. They change the way people live! Their ideas sweep across the world and leave the past behind them.

Yet, Jesus remains steadfast in the ways that He has done things. He still reaches into the hearts of the people, calling them to righteousness. He blesses every generation who takes up His cross and carries it to those who have an ear to hear. Jesus spans across the centuries with His message. His message remains true because it is the minds and actions of the people that count in society.

There are people who need guidance in all generations. No matter what their surroundings are, no matter how they may dress, it is their inner nature that needs to draw from the resources that Jesus gives. His destiny is still being fulfilled by every person who has discovered Him. His life is eternal and so are the lessons that His life teaches. He is never considered to be a stranger to life on earth. He is the ultimate example of what life can be. People can emulate His grace and mercy no matter when they live.

They Are in Control of Their Own Destiny and He Allows Them to Make a Free Choice

Who can understand his errors? cleanse thou me from secret faults. Keep back thy servant also from presumptuous sins; let them not have dominion over me: then shall I be upright, and I shall be innocent from the great transgression. Let the words of my mouth, and the meditation of my heart, be acceptable in thy sight, O LORD, my strength, and my redeemer.

(PSALM 19:12–14, KJV)

April 21, 1999

The words of my mouth and the meditation of my heart are on You, dear Jesus. Words can hurt! They can cause problems within families. Each word means something, and when Jesus is the source of the Word, the Word can become alive. It can cause great things to come to pass in the lives of the people.

There are also words that are spoken by those who are in authority that are not godly in any way. They are spoken to cause disruption in a society. It is in the interest of these leaders to cause disruption so that they can destroy their enemies. Their enemies can be anyone who disagrees with them.

A corrupt government will cause destruction among its own people in order to retain power. It will stop at nothing to become the sole governing power among its people. They do not care if justice is being done. They have their own form of justice and they will trample over the rights of innocent people to retain rulership over them.

Jesus rules in love. He lets the people who have called upon His name have the right to stand for what they believe. He will not corrupt them to make them His slaves. He, instead, gives them more freedom to do their own will. When they must choose the way they are to live their lives, He allows them the right to make up their own minds.

Jesus will not coerce them to follow Him! He has created people and He trusts them to make valid, righteous choices. He doesn't pressure them against their will. He does, when people call upon His name, teach them right from wrong. He does enrich their lives when they follow in His ways. He does let them know the price of the wages of sin. They are in control of their own destiny and He allows them to make a free choice.

When people are coerced, they are under pressure to do that which they do not want to do. In their minds they know that it will not benefit them, and they will do anything to escape confrontation. They do not want to battle against odds that can cause them problems.

Love Means Doing Something for Someone That May Be Inconvenient

Keep yourselves in the love of God, looking for the mercy of our Lord Jesus Christ unto eternal life. And of some have compassion, making a difference: And others save with fear, pulling them out of the fire; hating even the garment spotted by the flesh.

(JUDE 21–23, KJV)

April 22, 1999

Let there be glory, honor, and praises unto the Lord Jesus Christ. He has brought refinement to the people of earth. Because of Him, great societies have been raised up. The people were able to build and to provide justice for each other because Jesus gave them the peace needed to build a great society.

Whenever there is lawlessness, people worry about survival. They are able to care for themselves, but they do not have the support needed to build society in general. It is when people are taught that they are responsible for their fellow man and that the more people agree and work together, they have the ability to grow as a community.

The more people one can associate with, the more they are able to expand their influence. They are able to tap into others'

191

talents and resources, and use them for their own purposes and abilities. When people form nations they are becoming capable of defending themselves and their ideas. They have others who protect them from danger when they are not able to care for themselves. This means that people of all ages can enrich one another. A person can help others live a more joyous, full life when they support each other in a time of weakness.

Jesus wants people to love one another. Love means doing something for someone that may be inconvenient. They must share their time and money with those who cannot care for themselves. The more people care for each other, the more they are apt to find others who care for them in return!

It is when an evil society rises up that people become expendable. They have lived out their usefulness and there is no one who will care for them. They may be able to tell about when they were young and able to do as they pleased, but there is no one who really cares to hear. That selfish attitude makes people feel as if their lives were of little importance. They want other people to notice them. They want people to remember when they were of value to society in general!

If they didn't touch other people's lives, there will be few who can remember them. They restrained themselves and didn't want to bother with others; now there are few who remember them. It is a loveless society for them.

Jesus Is the True Center of All Life

All that the Father giveth me shall come to me; and him that cometh to me I will in no wise cast out. For I came down from heaven, not to do mine own will, but the will of him that sent me.

(*John 6:37–38, KJV*)

April 23, 1999

My soul escapes, like a bird out of the snare of the fowler! For I was lost but now I'm found. In Jesus, my life is renewed, and all that was stolen away from me has been returned. Jesus is the true center of all life. He has made it possible for the relationship God had with Adam and Eve to be restored once more.

We see Jesus, with all His mercy and kindness spread out before us. He brings hope when all hope has been taken from us. He brings love to souls who have forgotten what love really can be for them. He brings hope and joy in a hopeless, joyless world. Jesus is Lord of the soul; it is preserved for us by His love and tender mercies!

He is known as a man of sorrows. He came to earth to die. He was not allowed to know the joys that people enjoy. He didn't own "things"! He had no woman to call His own. He had no children of His own. Yet, everything belongs to Him. All the children in the world are His! He has the last word over all life. He blesses every-thing that lives because He lived.

We run after Jesus. We want what He has! We see Him as being holy before us. He is life and we want more life. We want Him to be everything in our lives and we ask Him to provide it for us. Even though these are the very things that He refused for Himself while He lived on Earth, we want Him to provide them for us.

"Give us this day our daily bread!" we pray, for we know that in food we support our life. "Forgive us our sins," for we know that we are sinners, but we continue in our sinful actions!

How are we supposed to connect with Jesus? For we love Him and we know He is true. That which He has provided for people is all that they will possibly need, but people want more. They want the riches of earth and the everlasting glory of Heaven and eternity.

We do come before you, Lord Jesus. Although the things on earth had very little draw for You, You still are our Provider. Life is in Your hands. As we see the changing seasons, we marvel at their beauty and the wisdom of the cycle of life. Help us to be in Your divine will. Do not let us be stolen from You. Keep us in Your ways!

WHAT DID JESUS KNOW THAT OTHER PEOPLE DID NOT?

Jesus, when he had cried again with a loud voice, yielded up the ghost. And, behold, the veil of the temple was rent in twain from the top to the bottom; and the earth did quake, and the rocks rent; And the graves were opened; and many bodies of the saints which slept arose, And came out of the graves after his resurrection, and went into the holy city, and appeared unto many.

(MATTHEW 27:50–53, KJV)

April 24, 1999

Thou art worthy, dear Jesus Christ, to bring glory, honor and praise unto God the Father. He has given that which is most precious for the sake of others. He is rich in mercy and has seen fit to trust God with His life. He willingly did that which God told him to do, even though it meant the end of His life upon the earth.

What did Jesus know that other people did not? To give up one's life when one is not sure what lies beyond death is a great chance for a person to take. But Jesus pressed forward, assured that there is life after death. He knew that as great as life on earth is for people, life that is after earthly death can still be greater.

It is difficult for people to grasp when there isn't anybody who has come back from death who can walk among us and relate what they have seen. There are instances in Scripture where one can get a small glimpse of life after death, but they seem too inconclusive for people to be able to build a sure route where one can really go!

People are restrained by the fear of life after death. If they are called to answer for their sins, then they will live a more holy life. If they think there are no consequences for their actions, they then would do anything that feels good to them. They would have no fear of living a self-centered life. They wouldn't have any regard for anyone except their own pleasure.

The reason there is so much sin upon earth is that people declare that they do not believe in an afterlife. Or they think that they have many opportunities to change the outcome of their eternal end by coming back to earth again and again. Surely, they reason, if there is an eternal God, He needs them to populate Heaven. What ruler wants to have just a few souls to lead when they need a world full of believers?

Jesus is our example that there is life after death. It is true that He is an exception to what the average person experiences after death. One does not see the newly departed walking upon earth talking to their friends. If one did, they would be more apt to believe in an after-death eternal life. We must take Jesus as our example and believe that we, too, have an eternal place where our Spirit lives on!

HE BECOMES THEIR STRENGTH IN TIMES OF TURMOIL!

And ye shall be hated of all men for my name's sake: but he that endureth to the end shall be saved. But when they perse- cute you in this city, flee ye into another: for verily I say unto you, Ye shall not have gone over the cities of Israel, till the Son of man be come. The disciple is not above his master, nor the servant above his lord.

(MATTHEW 10:22–24, KJV)

April 26, 1999

Come bless the Lord, all Ye children of the Lord! When times look desperate, that is the time to call upon Jesus and His ways. He is able to take care of all the needs of the people. He gives directions to those who call upon Him. He becomes their strength in times of turmoil!

All over the world the Christians are being persecuted by other people. They are not flexible enough for those who would cause sin to grow. There is much profit in sin. People do things to excess by doing wicked things; there is never enough income to feed one's habits. So the people who refuse to engage in selfish behav- ior and who live a conservative life are made outcasts by others.

People hate to be corrected! They call people who control themselves and who refuse to be extravagant, "Goody, goody two shoes!" It is supposed to make them loosen up and be more fun-loving. Other people enjoy seeing people make fools of themselves, while they remain in control of themselves.

People like gossip. They want to besmirch other people so that they, in turn, seem to be more important. There comes a time when people who seek after wickedness have their sins revealed to others. There is no chance of reversing the revelation of what they have done. They are held accountable for what they do.

Jesus could be humorous. Those who knew Him appreciated His sense of humor. He was kind to many people who were not kind to others. Jesus embraced those who found themselves in situations that were overcoming them. He told them how to handle the situation and to sin no more. Sin does bring trouble to people even if they are impervious to the fact that they were sinning.

One may think they are going down a two-way street, but they can be killed if they are going the wrong way on a one-way street. These accidents are not reversible. Trouble can cause much harm to those who declare ignorance in a situation—trouble that can be costly for them!

It Is Really Important When People Ask Jesus into Their Hearts

No man can come to me, except the Father which hath sent me draw him: and I will raise him up at the last day. It is written in the prophets, And they shall be all taught of God. Every man therefore that hath heard, and hath learned of the Father, cometh unto me.

(JOHN 6:44–45, KJV)

April 27, 1999

My soul escaped, like a bird out of the snare of the fowler! I give Thee thanks, dear Jesus, for making this so. For all people are born in spiritual ignorance, yet they have a chance to find moral righteousness when they live on earth. Do they all have a call to find Jesus and receive His blessings? Every person, through their culture, can learn what is right and what is wrong. It is up to them to seek and find their way unto Jesus.

Christianity has been around for a long time. There really isn't any excuse for people not to have heard about Jesus. If they have any curiosity at all, they will seek Him to find out what He is really all about. There is a drawing unto Jesus as each person's soul seeks that which is beneficial for themselves. Not all find Jesus, not all want what He has to offer.

It is really important when people ask Jesus into their hearts. They have made a confession that Jesus is Lord. When this happens, there can be a drawing unto Jesus in a more concentrated way. But it is in the power of people to move ahead with their lives in the manner that they have become accustomed. They can refuse the wooing of the Holy Spirit and go their way. There is no one who forces them to do anything. In fact, there are spiritual forces that are not of God that will hinder their progress toward a spiritual walk with Jesus!

Jesus is open for all to receive. They can go as far as they would like in their walk with Jesus. Jesus will call them; they can respond but they are never forced into changing their lifestyles. They can live as they please and die in their sins. Or they can search for that which will improve their lives and make life more enjoyable for them.

Jesus is rich in resources. The whole of the world lies before Him. He could have anything that He wanted in Heaven and earth. Yet, He has set His heart on the souls of the people so that they may be as He is. He doesn't think of Himself; He thinks about the people and what they could be, here and eternally.

Jesus is Lord, but He is a gentle Lord who puts His proposals out before the people. They are able to decide the way they will go. He will not force them into subjection unto Him!

The More Trust a Person Puts into Jesus, the More Like Him They Become

Trust in the LORD with all thine heart; and lean not unto thine own understanding. In all thy ways acknowledge him, and he shall direct thy paths.

(PROVERBS 3:5–6, KJV)

April 28, 1999

Jesus, Jesus, how I love Him! How I trust Him over and over! Jesus, Jesus, precious Jesus, oh for grace to trust Him more!

The more trust people put into Jesus, the more like Him they become. They learn that there is no one else whom they can confide in and feel as if they have been heard. Jesus does know each person personally. He is with them day and night. When people confess Jesus Christ as their Savior, they can become as one with Him.

There are those people who take Jesus lightly. They do not consider Him to be any more deity than any other one that people call god. They do not realize that Jesus is more than a deity! He is the only true God, and those who place their trust in Him will find peace and comfort. They will know without a doubt that there is no other beside Him. Jesus is Lord.

Those who ask Jesus into their hearts should see a tremendous change in themselves. They should hate evil and love goodness and truth. All the rest of the days of their lives should be spent in pursuing the truth and goodness of Him. There is no place that they can go where they won't carry Jesus with them. He lives in them; they abide in Him. They are reflections of His good nature. They are always assured that He brings good to them and not misadventure.

We claim that Jesus is our Lord. We know that He is with us at all times. We are aware of His precious presence, that He is supporting us in all that we do. We know that any evil deed on our side is an affront to Jesus. We cause Him to be embarrassed for us when we do not follow His teachings.

There isn't any Word that Jesus gives to us that we should doubt. We must remain steadfast in Him. He would never cause us any harm. It's our own foolishness that causes us to harm ourselves. Jesus can't support sin and sin leads to foolishness and wickedness.

Can foolishness and wickedness lead to a Christian's destruction? Yes, people live in a wicked world where they become used to seeing sin abound. But Jesus places strength in His people to overcome any sin that is in the world. It's found in them who have the Holy Spirit and a desire to follow in Jesus' ways!

People Prospered as They Learned to Use What They Had About Them

The earth is the LORD's, and the fulness thereof; the world, and they that dwell therein. For he hath founded it upon the seas, and established it upon the floods. Who shall ascend into the hill of the LORD? or who shall stand in his holy place?

(PSALM 24:1–3, KJV)

April 29, 1999

All over the world, God's Spirit is moving! All over the world, like the prophet said it would be. The more the Spirit of God moves across the face of the earth, the more evilness rises up in rebellion against goodness.

One would declare that this statement is not true. When there are good and righteous people abounding on Earth, evil must be put away. People do not tolerate sin to flourish. A righteous people hate sin, and they fight against any sin that comes upon them.

But at this time the people become confused about right or wrong. There are those who consider certain actions to be too harsh. They feel that the people must be more tolerant toward others. They would treat each person equally. They want each person to have the same amount of value as someone else. Only when each person is equal in all things, will justice be done.

There are those who disagree! They think if a person is ambitious and has certain intelligence, they should be able to go as far as they want to go. If they show themselves prudent, they should get all that they have been able to earn. No one should stop them from accessing anything that they are able to earn.

Who is right? The person who feels that each person should receive exactly the same thing? Or an energetic person who is able to amass as much as they want? For each person would live as comfortably as they want to live. It isn't anyone's fault if one is not able to supply every person with exactly the same things.

God created the heavens and the earth. He made the earth diversified so that various parts of it supplied different things. Some places are hot, some are cold, and some are in between. Some are wet, some are dry, and some are in between. He let people go where they wanted to go. They could choose where they wanted to be.

Then He allowed mankind to learn how to survive on Earth in any manner that they had the capacity to live. The earth was theirs to do with as they pleased. The earth was neither good nor bad. People prospered as they learned to use what they had about them. But the greatness of people is the way that they have learned to deal with what they have and the way that they use their own resources.

Jesus Encourages People to Think for Themselves

And he causeth all, both small and great, rich and poor, free and bond, to receive a mark in their right hand, or in their foreheads: And that no man might buy or sell, save he that had the mark, or the name of the beast, or the number of his name. Here is wisdom. Let him that hath understanding count the number of the beast: for it is the number of a man; and his number is Six hundred threescore and six.

(REVELATION 13:16–18, KJV)

April 30, 1999

Let God arise and His enemies be scattered! Let righteousness be spread across the whole nation! Let people find tolerance with one another. Let there be room for all!

There is but One true Creator, and He is Jesus Christ. He made people in His image. He has given them great gifts and He gave them the world to govern. Until now, people have never had the ability to create a one-world government. Now, there is enough technology for people to rise up and rule from distant lands. We see the possibilities for control of people everywhere.

The average person cannot understand what is taking place about them. They do not know of the plans of the leaders who want to rule in a kingly manner. They may speak of equality for all people, but they are thinking mainly of themselves. They have no intentions of giving up their power to others. They would control the world with their strengths.

Death means little to them! People are the ones who the rulers want to control, but the people who rebel against them are expendable. They have too many others they can control to be concerned about those people who would serve another Master.

Jesus beckons people unto Him, not for His own glory but for righteousness sake. He would treat all people equally; He knows the people's strengths and weaknesses. He does not try to steal from them that which they have. He helps build their weakness so that they are strong and able to conquer the problems that they have in life.

Jesus encourages people to think for themselves. He gives them discernment concerning their difficulties. He reaches down into their souls, and He shows them that they are precious and able to bring goodness to a dark world. No matter where a person lives, the message that Jesus gives can help anyone who asks of Him. He speaks to them in a way that they understand. At all times, He allows them to choose the way they will live their lives.

There is a spirit of the times. This spirit seeps into the minds and souls of the people. They become blinded to the truth of a certain matter. They will seek with great fervor those things that are not in their true interest. This spirit is not sent from Jesus. Jesus helps His people discern the spirit of the times!

INDEX

Book v, 85, 86, 113, 114, 132, 141, 161
Book of Life 113, 114, 161
Boring 14, 188
Born 7, 41, 56, 57, 80, 83, 85, 122, 140, 161, 163, 169, 199
Bothered 33, 55
Bound 22, 125, 155, 179
Bounty 20, 70
Bow 24, 48, 63, 72, 73, 81, 119, 176, 181
Brave 61
Brazen 17
Bread 27, 35, 73, 91, 161, 163, 194
Breadbasket 20
Breaking 29, 38, 60, 65, 66, 106, 125, 127, 128, 133, 150, 157, 184
Breathed 23
Brothers 8, 124
Build 48, 54, 129, 130, 156, 191, 196, 206
Builders 140
Bullies 22
Burden 18, 26, 41, 62, 98, 136, 145, 181
Burdensome 26, 136
Burn 2, 54
Buys 72

C

Calf 129
Call v, 5, 6, 12, 15, 16, 18, 25, 26, 42, 48, 49, 53, 54, 57, 66, 112, 114, 119, 120, 136, 176, 179, 182, 190, 193, 197, 199-201
Calm 77
Captive 63, 149, 152, 179
Captured 76
Cared 11, 39, 83, 118, 146, 166
Careful 30, 131, 142, 171, 172
Caring 11, 39, 72, 106, 146
Carpenter 166
Carry 13, 62, 81, 88, 139, 140, 180, 181, 202
Case 32, 42, 64, 65, 91, 185
Cast 8, 22, 30, 46, 47, 49, 67, 87, 93, 145, 155, 161, 193
Catch 69, 188
Caught 17, 27, 29, 34, 66, 128, 134, 141, 150, 157, 160
Cause 15, 16, 19, 22, 24, 28, 31, 47, 48, 52, 57, 62, 72, 75, 77, 89, 93, 94, 97, 107, 108, 126, 130, 133, 138, 146, 150, 156, 162, 170, 174, 182, 189, 190, 197, 198, 202, 205
Center 9, 16, 30, 193
Century 164
Chains 49

Challenges 80, 92
Chance 19, 27, 48, 78, 97, 98, 118, 122, 155, 158, 195, 198, 199
Change v, 2, 8, 14, 21, 24, 38, 44, 50-52, 56, 59, 60, 61, 72, 74, 77, 88, 92, 97, 114, 115, 120, 132, 144, 145, 150, 159, 160, 162, 163, 168, 170, 171, 174, 180, 182, 188, 196, 202
Character 8, 36, 54, 74, 85, 90, 98, 100, 109, 136, 140, 144, 147, 148, 158-160, 182
Charity 99, 110
Chart 59
Chase 36, 48
Cheated 94, 148
Cheek 156
Cheering 62
Child ix, 9, 10, 31, 36, 57, 79, 105, 106, 132, 171, 172
Childhood 9
Childish 31
Children vii, 7, 9, 10, 11, 16, 23, 31, 32, 49, 51, 54, 56, 63, 68, 71, 75, 81, 82, 99, 101, 105, 131, 132, 137-139, 144, 147, 153, 162, 166, 171, 172, 180, 187, 193, 197
Choice 22, 24, 28, 90, 130, 153, 164, 189, 190
Christ vii, 5, 6, 8, 16, 19, 20, 24, 26, 35, 73, 75, 83, 85, 93, 94, 99, 101, 102, 109, 113, 117, 121, 125, 131, 135, 143, 145, 147, 149, 177, 183, 185, 186, 191, 195, 201, 205
Chronic 66
Circumstances 6, 90, 102
Clamor 17, 42
Cleanse 22, 79, 189
Cleansing 50, 144
Clearly ix, 7, 122, 160, 176
Cleave 25
Cloaked 33
Closer v, 51, 76, 132
Clothes 46, 47, 107
Cloud 66, 119
Code 38, 72, 158, 173, 174
Code of ethics 38, 72, 174
Cold 61, 62, 204
Collision 38
Combat 32
Comfort 47, 118, 136, 179, 201
Comfortable 13, 72, 154
Comforter 21
Commandment 11, 25, 89, 90, 107, 129, 169, 170, 185
Commit 7, 27, 141, 150, 163, 184
Commodity 105
Common 13, 14, 55, 61, 66, 111, 133, 142

Lift 37, 39, 40, 85, 110, 137, 149, 153, 183
Lifted 68, 85
Light 1, 23, 30, 65, 89, 125, 154, 163, 185
Likeminded 101
Limits 142
Linen 123
Lips 75, 181
Listen 10, 36, 37, 58, 135, 143, 171
Lose 6, 24, 27, 36, 39, 48, 134, 168
Loses 95, 103, 130, 172
Loss 51, 106, 110, 156
Lost vii, 14, 20, 22, 29, 33, 56, 100, 117, 144, 148, 156, 167, 193
Love v, vi, 9-11, 13, 15, 22, 25, 29, 30, 31, 36, 39, 44, 53, 54, 74, 75, 79, 81, 83, 89, 93, 97, 99, 100, 102, 105, 106, 111, 118, 119, 123, 124, 127, 135, 138, 145, 148, 149, 155, 156, 159, 160, 163, 165-167, 169, 171-173, 186, 187, 190-194, 201, 202
Love match 79
Lukewarm 61, 62
Lust 127, 130, 157, 168
Luxury 186
Lying 2, 33, 66

M

Magnificent 79
Majority 67, 96, 178
Maker 24
Malfeasance 34
Malice 35
Man vi, 7, 12, 29, 31, 39, 42, 43, 46, 74, 83, 84, 88, 98, 99, 109, 111, 113, 115, 127, 132, 133, 136, 141, 159, 161, 163, 165-167, 173, 184, 185, 187, 191, 193, 197, 199, 205
Manifest 7
Manipulate 9, 167
Mankind v, vii, 7, 24, 41, 42, 44, 59, 68, 83, 84, 107-109, 111, 116, 120, 123, 125, 135, 146-149, 161, 166, 175, 180, 204
Man-made 38, 170
Mannerism 92
Marauding 76
Mark 39, 65, 71, 87, 205
Market 44
Marriage 13, 14, 123, 124
Marry 13, 159
Martyrs 47, 48
Marvelous 76, 80, 83, 131, 154, 174
Mass destruction 78
Masses 50, 88, 170

Mass murder 50
Master 5, 93, 176, 197, 206
Mastermind 180
Mate 14
Mating 83
Matters v, 27, 42, 43, 51, 52, 94, 96, 100, 116, 118, 120, 166, 182
Mayhem 158
Memories 86
Mention 5, 142, 156
Mercy 46, 49, 76, 121, 126, 138, 167, 188, 191, 193, 195
Message 24, 25, 61, 67, 70, 88, 118, 132, 143, 170, 188, 206
Messiah 88, 165
Mighty 5, 19, 121, 122, 132
Mighty God 57
Mind v, 2, 7, 15, 16, 18, 19, 24, 31, 50-52, 66, 77, 81, 84, 85, 89, 99, 101, 102, 112, 126, 128, 131, 132, 136, 138, 146, 148, 150, 156, 174, 175, 181-184, 188, 190, 206
Mindless 80
Mindset 6, 50
Miracle 12, 83
Miracles ix, 12, 76
Mischief 33
Misdeeds 34
Miserable 45, 103, 130, 143, 144
Misleading 34
Misrepresentation 34
Mistake 10, 112
Misunderstood 85, 144
Misuse 54
Mobilized 76
Mock 67
Mockery 16
Model 90
Monetary 30, 94
Money 14, 18, 47, 70-72, 77, 93, 94, 109, 110, 182, 184, 185, 192
Moral 8, 21, 26, 62, 72, 80, 88, 94, 116, 147-149, 157, 158, 199
Moral cause 62
Morals 152
Mordecai 107
More 1, 5, 7, 8, 11, 17, 18, 20, 21, 25, 26, 32, 34, 36, 39, 44, 65, 71, 74, 76, 81, 83, 88, 91, 92, 94, 98, 102, 104, 108, 111, 115, 120, 122, 126, 130, 132, 136, 142, 163, 167, 168, 171, 176, 178-180, 184-186, 190-194, 196-198, 200, 201, 203
Moses 25, 139, 140, 141, 151, 169, 170

Remission 135
Remnants 80
Remorseful 24
Remove 2, 15, 23, 26, 74, 80
Removed 18, 91
Renewed 60, 179, 193
Repel 63
Repentance 24, 63, 65, 135, 150
Repercussion 34
Reporting 29
Reproach 55, 74, 178
Reproduce 84
Repulsed 22, 32, 77
Reputation 173
Rescue 12
Resent 21
Resentment 67, 156
Resentments 155, 156
Reserve 12, 78, 157
Reserved 49, 86
Resist 21, 52, 67, 129, 159, 175
Resolution 2
Resolved 60, 156, 182
Resources 20, 188, 192, 200, 204
Respect 13, 18, 93, 107, 108, 110, 139, 140, 142, 170, 172
Respects 18
Respite 168
Responsibility 10, 12, 38, 72, 146, 150
Responsible 10, 18, 152, 156, 157, 182, 191
Restore 14-16, 76, 119
Restrained 100, 192, 196
Resurrection 121, 195
Revelation 13, 61, 113, 117, 123, 198, 205
Reverse 26, 144, 182
Reversible 198
Revisions 60
Revolted 32
Reward 15, 18, 93
Rhetoric 17
Ride 49, 63, 132
Right 5, 10, 18, 20, 25, 26, 28,-30, 38, 50, 58, 67, 68, 73, 77, 82, 91, 96, 98, 100, 106, 108, 112, 115, 125, 130, 139, 142, 143, 154, 159, 160, 164, 173, 176, 178, 190, 199, 203, 204, 205
Righteous 7, 8, 16-18, 35, 57, 65, 67, 79, 80, 110, 115, 122, 142, 144, 145, 176, 190, 203
Righteousness 7, 8, 15, 16, 18, 21, 22, 25, 26, 29, 30, 33, 36, 37, 41, 49, 50-52, 58, 62, 64, 74, 77, 80, 86, 89, 90, 95, 102, 112, 114-116, 122, 123, 127, 129, 130, 137, 168,

176, 178, 179, 183, 187, 188, 199, 205, 206
Rights 50, 65, 66, 68, 125, 170, 190
Rise 78, 80, 95, 111, 113, 118, 135, 147, 178, 180, 192, 203, 205
Risen 55, 155, 179, 185
Rock 9, 11, 105, 159, 167, 173, 195
Romans 37, 101, 143, 167, 170, 183
Rooftops 61
Rooted 54
Roots 86
Rope 18
Ruin 30, 64, 160
Rule 9, 17, 20, 26, 75, 76, 78, 94, 100, 117, 122, 170, 205
Ruled 16, 86, 106
Rulers 37, 64, 86, 140, 185, 206
Rulership 190
Rules 6, 17, 18, 90, 94, 116, 144, 158, 190
Ruse 14
Rust 55

S

Sackcloth 107
Sacred 10
Sacrifice 28, 118, 123, 124, 126, 143, 150, 173, 174
Safety 9, 95, 108, 170
Salt 1
Salvation 5, 9, 11, 101, 102, 105, 124, 135, 137, 140, 150, 159, 162, 165, 167, 173
Same 13, 18, 32, 34, 39, 45, 56, 59, 60, 69, 78, 84, 101, 102, 104, 118, 120, 146, 148, 150, 152, 162-164, 168, 170, 174, 184, 203, 204
Samuel 147
Sanctuary 137, 153
Santa Claus 11
Satisfaction 43, 47, 81, 103
Satisfied 30, 43, 74, 175
Saul 47
Save 1, 6, 39, 42, 46, 75, 79, 144, 148, 152, 162, 191, 205
Saved 2, 8, 41, 49, 69, 99, 112, 143, 150, 167, 197
Saving 24, 148
Savior 35, 42, 45, 60, 88, 103, 114, 119, 147, 151, 161, 201
Scattered 57, 205
Scenario 164
School 10
Schools 140

CPSIA information can be obtained
at www.ICGtesting.com
Printed in the USA
LVHW032305281118
598463LV00009B/64/P

9 781595 558275